HARVARD SQUARE.

The Cambridge of 1776

Mary Williams Greely

HERITAGE BOOKS
2008

HERITAGE BOOKS
AN IMPRINT OF HERITAGE BOOKS, INC.

Books, CDs, and more—Worldwide

For our listing of thousands of titles see our website
at
www.HeritageBooks.com

Published 2008 by
HERITAGE BOOKS, INC.
Publishing Division
100 Railroad Avenue, Suite 104
Westminster, Maryland 21157-4826

Originally published 1875

All rights reserved. No part of this book may be reproduced or transmitted in any form or by any means, electronic or mechanical, including photocopying, recording or by any information storage and retrieval system without written permission from the author, except for the inclusion of brief quotations in a review.

International Standard Book Number: 978-07884-3026-8

Theatrum Majorum.

The Cambridge of 1776:

Wherein is set forth an Account of the Town, and of the
Events it Witnessed:

WITH WHICH IS INCORPORATED

THE DIARY OF DOROTHY DUDLEY,

Now first publish'd;

Together with an *Historicall Sketch*; Severall Appropriate
POEMS; Numerous Anecdotes, patriotick, weighty,
indifferent, and diverting; Many References to *the* RENOWNED UNIVERSITY;
and *Descriptions of the People
of the Olden Time.*

All of which is adapted to the furtherance of *Good Manners,
Virtue, Piety, Intelligence, Love of Country, and*
ADMIRATION OF CAMBRIDGE.

Done by Divers Eminent Hands, and

Edited for the

Ladies Centennial Committee by A. G.

*Hic manus, ob patriam pugnando vulnera passi
Quique pii vates, et Phœbo digna locuti:
Inventas aut qui vitam excoluere per artes,
Quique sui memores alios fecere merendo.* — VIRG.

Quæ fugiunt, celeri carpite poma manu. — OVID.

Adorned with Cuts and a Map.

CAMBRIDGE:

*Printed on the Site of Fort Number One: Over against the
Town of Brighton, on the River's Side. To be sold in Boston by Lockwood, Brooks, and Company, on Washington and
Bromfield Streets.*

M D CCC LXX VI.

☞ The Ladies find that the Latin title of this Volume contains an Intimation that the Book is a *Stage* on which our Ancestors (those who have "gone over to the Majority") are the Actors.

The Quotation from Virgil proves to have been taken from a Description of *Elysium*, and is therefore eminently appropriate in its place. One learned in tongues translates it thus: "Here is a Company of Heroes who were wounded fighting for their Country; of pious Bards who sung in strains worthy of Apollo; of those who have improved human Life by the Arts they have invented; and those who have by their services made other men cherish their memory."

The Line from Ovid conveys the following admonition: "Pluck with quick Hand the Fruit that is passing away."

Organization of the Ladies' Centennial Committee, of Cambridge, Mass.

    Mrs. THOMAS P. JAMES, *Chairman*.
    Mrs. J. GARDNER WHITE, *Treasurer*.
    Miss ALICE M. LONGFELLOW, *Secretary*.

Mrs. ANSON BURLINGAME.	Mrs. GEORGE LIVERMORE.
Mrs. HENRY DEXTER.	Mrs. HENRY W. PAINE.
Miss MARY FELTON.	Miss MARY L. PARMENTER.
Mrs. JOHN M. FISKE.	Mrs. SAMUEL B. RINDGE.
Mrs. C. L. HARDING.	Mrs. GEORGE P. SANGER.
Mrs. HENRY O. HOUGHTON.	Mrs. EMORY WASHBURN.

Editor for the Committee, ARTHUR GILMAN, M. A.

Copyright, 1875,
By MARY WILLIAMS GREELY.

Advertisement to the Reader,

For the better Illustration and Understanding of this Book.

GENTLE READER:—This little Book is the Fruit of a *Labour of Love*, for which the Writers receive no Reward but that filial Satisfaction which must fill the virtuous Heart after having made an earnest Effort to do *Honour to the Memory of the Fathers*, and to depict the Nobility they displayed in the Struggle for Liberty.

The plan of commemorating our venerated Ancestors in this way (and of drawing a few Dollars into the Treasury of the Ladies' Centennial Committee of Cambridge), first suggested itself to *Mrs. George Livermore*. It was promptly adopted by the Committee, and the Work was delegated to the present Editor. He was gratified to find a general Interest in the Project, and the Papers comprising this Volume were obtained within a few Weeks.

The wish of the Editor, and his Co-laborers, has been to present a Picture of *The Cambridge of* 1776; putting the Reader in Possession of such Facts as would enable him to realize the Feelings of our Fathers; to see the Streets they trod, the Churches in which they worshipped, the Houses in which they dwelt; and, in some Measure, *to appreciate the Trials they unflinchingly endured.*

It is thought that this little Book will be found very pleasant for all the People of Cambridge to read, and most necessary to remember. What, indeed, would we not give for such a Volume written by our Fathers of 1776, about their Fathers of 1676? What will tempt our Children of 1976 to part with the Copies which (after committing their Contents to Memory) we shall *bestow in our Atticks* to await the Morn of their hundredth Year?

But the Editor believes that this *Memoir of the Olden Time* will possess an Interest for many Thousands beyond the Limits of Cambridge, whose Ancestors fought in the Revolution, as well as for all who rejoice in the Liberty then made sure. Can Words or Figures express the Value of a true Record of a Town famed as *the first Campground of the Revolution;* renowned for its ancient University; and known the world over for its Poets, Historians, Novelists, Men of Science, and of State-craft, — its Winthrops, Vassalls, Brattles, Belchers; its Kirkland, Sparks, Everett, Felton, Agassiz; its Longfellow,[1] Lowell, Holmes, Howells; its Peabody, Abbot, Child; — men who will ever wear Laurels that cannot fade?

It can be said of our beloved Home that its every natural Trait has been celebrated in Prose or Verse. Not to enter into Detail, it may be mentioned that *Mr. Longfellow* has immortalized its Village Smithy, and its Head-quarters of Washington; *Dr. Holmes* and *Mr. Lowell* have celebrated its Graveyard, its Marshes, its River, its Sidewalks and Trees, even the very Dust of its Streets,[2] and *Mr. Howells* sends its Horse-cars down the Track of the Ages to the perpetual Delectation of our Children's Children.

When *Samuel Purchas, Master of Arts,* set forth his Book entitled, "A Theatre of Politicall Flying Insects, accompanied by Three Centuries of Observations Theologicall and Morall, drawn from the Nature, the Worth, the Work and the Wonder of *the Bee,*" he used Words which the present Editor adopts as his own. "*Embroiderers,*" said Purchas, "*of Threds of divers Colors make a costly and delightful Hanging: So Writers out of a Thousand Parcels, an uniform and agreeing Body; whom I have labored to imitate. Where I have failed pardon my Weakness, and accept my good will.*"

The Ladies and their Servant, the Editor, desire to express their cordial *Thanks*

To President Eliot; Messrs. F. O. Vaille and H. A. Clarke, Editors of the "Harvard Book;" Mr. S. A. Drake; Messrs. J. R. Osgood & Co., and Messrs. H. O. Houghton & Co., for the free Use of the Cuts with which the Volume is adorned;

To Mr. Sibley, for Courtesies received at the College Library;

---

[1] "Long days be his, and each as lusty-sweet,
    As gracious natures find his song to be;
    May Age steal on with softly-cadenced feet,
    Falling in music, as for time were meet,
        Whose choicest verse is harsher-toned than he!"—*Lowell.*

[2] See page 110.

Advertisement to the Reader.

To the Librarian of the Essex Institute, at Salem, for similar kind Attentions ;

To Mrs. M. C. Sparks, Miss C. L. Donnison, Miss Mary Howe, and Others for the Use of valuable Letters ;

To the present Occupants of the ancient Houses, for Permission to visit and describe them ;

To Mr. Longfellow, Mr. Lowell, and Dr. Holmes, for their kind Permission to use the Extracts from their Poems, which are to be found in the Volume ;

To Dr. Peabody, Mr. Howells, Mr. John Holmes, Mr. Scudder, Mr. Haskins, Mr. Lathrop, Mrs. Folsom, and Mrs. James, for their Contributions ;

To Miss Mary Williams Greely, for the *untiring Diligence, and sympathetic Zeal* with which she has laboured in consulting historical Authorities and in verifying all the Details of the entertaining Diary of Dorothy Dudley, and in preparing it for the Press ;

To Mr. Charles Deane, for his valuable Aid in the Verification of important Facts and Dates, and in the Examination of a large Portion of the Manuscript of this Book ;

To Mr. Justin A. Jacobs, the long-time City clerk, for valuable Aid ;

To the Reverend Lucius R. Paige, for Information and Suggestions ;[1]

To Miss Mary Isabella James, for collating Authorities, and preparing the Map which illustrates the Volume ; and

To Messrs. Lockwood, Brooks, & Co., Booksellers in Boston, for kindly offering to sell this Book without the usual Commissions.

It only remains to add that this Memoir is

DEDICATED
TO THE PEOPLE OF CAMBRIDGE
OF 1976.

CAMBRIDGE, *Thanksgiving Day*, 1875.

---

[1] The Editor understands that Mr. Paige has for Years had in Preparation a History of Cambridge, the Appearance of which is looked for with much Interest.

The Table

Of the Contents of this Book.

	PAGE
I. *Sonnet. — Dorothy Dudley. By William D. Howells*	1
II. *Sketch of the History of Cambridge from its Settlement in 1631 to 1776. By David Greene Haskins, Jr.*	3
III. *The Influence of Cambridge in the Formation of the Nation. By Andrew P. Peabody, D. D.*	12
IV. *Extracts from the Diary of Dorothy Dudley, from April 18th, 1775, to July 19th, 1776.*	

The Battle of Lexington, p. 18 — The Army gathers on Cambridge Common, p. 20 — Citizens leave Boston, p. 21 — Ticonderoga, p. 22 — Gage offers Pardon to all but Adams and Hancock, p. 23 — Battle of Bunker Hill 24

Washington appointed Commander-in-chief, p. 25 — His Appearance in Cambridge, p. 26 — Fast Day, p. 27 — Aaron Burr — Letter to Miss Livingstone, p. 28 — Cambridge described, p. 29 — Dr. Appleton and his poultry, p. 31 — John Hancock and Dorothy Quincy, p. 32 — The Vassall Houses, p. 34 — The Expedition to Quebec, p. 36 — Dr. Franklin in Cambridge, p. 37 — The Traitor Church 38

Raising a new Army, p. 40 — British Ships captured, p. 41 — Mrs. John Adams in Cambridge — Society at Major Mifflin's, p. 42 — Gen. Lee and his Dog — Crime in Camp — Letter from Washington, p. 43 — Mrs. Washington arrives in Cambridge — Distress of the Army . . . 44

Sketch of Harvard College, pp. 44-48 — The first Graduate, p. 44 — Eaton, and his Misdeeds, p. 45 — President Dunster, p. 45 — Rules of the College — Library increased, 46 — The College visited in 1680, p. 47 — Other Presidents — Harvard Hall burned 48

Christ Church opened for Service, p. 49 — The Congregation of former Days described, 50 — Union Flag raised on Prospect Hill, p. 51 — The Colonists more than ever united, p. 52 — Faneuil Hall desecrated — Friendly Indians in Cambridge, p. 63 — Paine's "Common Sense" issued 54

The unsuccessful Expedition to Quebec, p. 55 — A reception by Mrs. Washington — Original letter of Washington, p. 56 — Games of Chance

Table of Contents.

prohibited by Washington, p. 57 — The Soldiers' Rations — Desire of Washington to attack Boston, p. 58 — Dorchester Heights occupied — Fast Day appointed, p. 59 — Boston evacuated by Gen. Howe — Boston open to All, p. 60 — Washington congratulated by Congress, p. 61 — He attends the "Thursday Lecture" — Leaves Cambridge 62

Miss Dudley visits Boston, p. 63 — The Hancock House, p. 64 — King's Chapel — North Church, p. 65 — Copp's Hill — Gov. Hutchinson's Mansion, p. 66 — People of Note in Cambridge in 1776, p. 67 — Affairs in Boston, again, p. 70 — Dr. Byles 71

A drive through Cambridge, p. 72 — The Meeting-House, Court-House, p. 73 — President's House, Wigglesworth House, Butler's Hill, Inman House, p. 74 — Phipps House, Bradish Tavern, Brattle House, p. 75 — The five College Buildings, Hastings House, The Whitefield Elm, p. 76 — Church or Tory Row, Belcher House, Vassall House, p. 77 — Sewall House, Lee House, p. 78 — Ruggles or Fayerweather House, Oliver House 79

Cambridge anticipates the Declaration of Independence, p. 80 — British Fleet leaves Boston, p. 81 — Students return from Concord, p. 82 — July 3d, 1776, p. 83 — Letters of Edmund Quincy, p. 84 — Independence declared 87

V. The Guests at Head-Quarters. By H. E. Scudder . . . 89
VI. The Batchelder House, and its Owners. By Mrs. Isabella James 93
VII. English Letter describing the Battle of Lexington. Contributed by Mrs. M. C. Sparks 103
VIII. Letters of Edmund Quincy. Contributed by Miss Donnison . . 106
IX. Verses on the Scenery of Cambridge. By Mr. Lowell and Dr. Holmes 110
X. The Old Court House. By John Holmes 111
XI. Lament of the Weathercock of 1776. By Mrs. Charles Folsom . 115
XII. Praise of the Past. By George Parsons Lathrop 117
XIII. Partial List of Authorities consulted in Preparing this Book . . 119
XIV. Index 121

List of Illustrations.

I.	The Harvard Square of 1776	Frontispiece.
II.	Map of the Cambridge of 1776	2
III.	The Congregational Church	11
IV.	The Washington Elm	13
V.	The Old President's House	16
VI.	Portrait of General Joseph Warren	19
VII.	The Old Parsonage, built in 1670	30
VIII.	Portrait of Samuel Adams	33
IX.	Cannon used before Boston	41
X.	Hessian Flag	52
XI.	Second Harvard Hall, built in 1766	54
XII.	Hollis Hall, completed in 1763	61
XIII.	The Wigglesworth House	73
XIV.	Holden Chapel	76
XV.	The Sewall-Riedesel Mansion	78
XVI.	Stoughton Hall. (Taken down in 1780)	81
XVII.	The Brattle Arms	90
XVIII.	The Belcher Arms	95

Dorothy Dudley

Fair maiden, whom a hundred summers keep
   Forever seventeen, and whose dark locks
   Are whitened only from the powder-box,
After those many winters: on the steep
Of high-heeled shoes, and with the silken sweep
   Of quaint brocade, and an arch smile that mocks
   At Time's despite, thy lovely semblance walks,
This year, our continent from deep to deep
   At numberless Centennial Tea-Parties,
   With chicken-salad, coffee, chocolate,
For retrospective youth, whose bosoms swell
   When they behold thee and thy pleasing freight,
   With love of country, and each patriot sees
Thy charm in all that thou dost chronicle.

                        W. D. Howells.

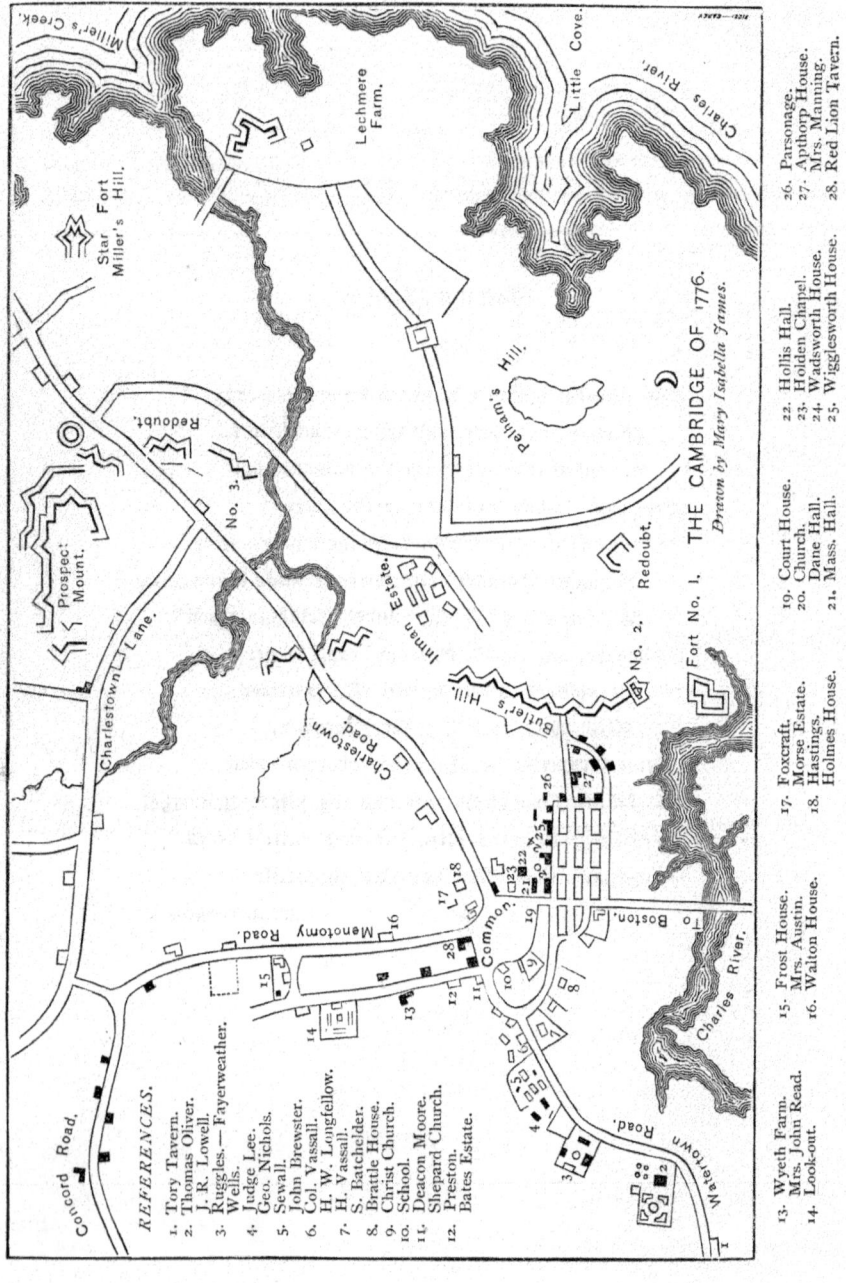

THE CAMBRIDGE OF 1776.

SKETCH OF THE HISTORY OF CAMBRIDGE FROM ITS SETTLEMENT IN 1631 TO 1776.

BY DAVID GREENE HASKINS, JR.

IN the year 1630, under the auspices of the Massachusetts Bay Company, a large fleet of English ships spread its sails for the shores of New England; and about one thousand colonists, with John Winthrop, the Governor, and Thomas Dudley, the Deputy-Governor of the Company, and other gentlemen of respectability and of influence in its councils, settled at Dorchester, Charlestown, Boston, Watertown, Roxbury, Medford, and Lynn.[1] The hitherto struggling Colony was thus placed on a secure foundation. After providing shelter for the winter, one of the earliest objects of care was to select a site for a fortified capital city, where the settlers might be safe from the attacks of their Indian neighbors and of possible foreign invaders. After many consultations, a spot was at last chosen near the Charles river, about a mile below Watertown, and on the 28th of December the Governor, Deputy-Governor, and all but two of the assistants, bound themselves to build houses there in the spring and to remove thither their "ordnance and munition." Under such favorable auspices, early in 1631 the "Newe Towne" was begun. Houses were erected and a canal was made to connect the town with the river. But this prosperity was soon partially blighted. Amicable relations having been established with the neighboring Indians, the need of a fortified town was no longer strongly felt; most of the assistants failed to perform their agreement; and before winter the Governor, without consulting his associates, removed the frame of his unfinished house from Newtown to Boston, whose commercial facilities were greater, and whose people were anxious to retain him amongst them. Dudley resented this conduct, and it was probably one of the reasons which,

[1] Dudley's Letter to the Countess of Lincoln.

the next year, induced him to tender a resignation of his office ; but he was finally reconciled to the Governor through the efforts of several of the ministers.

Boston became the capital, but Newtown was not abandoned, though Dudley and Bradstreet alone of the magistrates adhered to their agreement to settle there. The town was surrounded, in 1632, at the common expense, with a palisade and fosse about a mile and a half in length,[1] running along the north side of the present Cambridge Common, and enclosing over a thousand acres. Traces of the fosse were visible at the beginning of this century.[2]

In August, a small band of colonists from the vicinity of Braintree, Essex County, England, by order of the Court, removed to Newtown from Mount Wollaston, where they had begun to settle. A church was built with a bell, which afterwards gave place for a time to a drum as a means of summoning the people ; but the town had no settled minister until the arrival of the Rev. Thomas Hooker. This eminent divine, at the earnest solicitation of the Braintree people, his friends and former hearers, had left his church in Holland, whither he had fled from persecution for non-conformity in England. Passing through the latter country at considerable personal risk, he succeeded in eluding pursuit, and sailed for America, where he arrived September 4, 1633, on the ship *Griffin*, together with his friend, the Rev. Samuel Stone, and the wealthy John Haynes. Mr. Hooker had been a preacher of great note at Chelmsford, near Braintree, in Essex, and fully sustained his reputation in this country, being styled by Cotton Mather, "the light of the Western churches." October 11, 1633, he and Mr. Stone were solemnly ordained pastor and teacher of the Newtown church, the eighth which was gathered in the Colony. It may be feared that his popularity might have been less, had he lived in a later age, for we read that on a Sunday afternoon, before Governor Winthrop and a very large congregation, he preached over two hours "to very good purpose."[3] Though numbering scarcely fifty families at this time,[4] it was not long before the Newtown people wearied of their narrow limits and complained that they had not sufficient meadow land for their cattle. After sending exploring parties to Agawam, Merrimack, and the Connecticut river, they asked leave, at the General Court sitting at Newtown, September, 1634, to remove to the last named region. The debate lasted several days. The petitioners pleaded, beside other arguments, "the strong bent of their spirits to remove." The opponents of the measure advanced considerations of expediency and religion against this "removing of a candlestick." The vote was taken. The magistrates and deputies, the two bodies composing the General Court, disagreed. The latter strenuously contested the right of the former to a

[1] Wood's *New England's Prospect*, p. 43.
[2] Holmes's *History of Cambridge*, p. 9, note.
[3] Winthrop's *History of New England*, vol. i. p. 304.
[4] Holmes's *History of Cambridge*, p. 10, note.

negative voice. The Court adjourned, and a special day of humiliation, in consequence of the difficulty, was kept throughout the Colony. The matter was temporarily settled by the consent of Mr. Hooker's people to remain and to receive grants of land on the south side of the Charles river.

They soon, however, became restless again, and, although at the General Court held at Newtown, May 6, 1635, John Haynes, one of their chief men, was elected governor, they resolved, apparently with the tacit consent of the Court, to follow "the strong bent of their spirits," and remove to the Connecticut, whither their neighbors of Dorchester and Watertown were also on the point of emigrating. They accordingly sold their estates to the Rev. Thomas Shepard and his company, who arrived at Boston in the ship *Defence*, October 3, 1635. This " holy, heavenly, sweet-affecting, and soul-ravishing minister,"[1] who had not yet completed his thirtieth year, had been a non-conformist clergyman in Essex County and elsewhere, and, after numerous perils by land and water, had succeeded in escaping from England, it is said in disguise and under an assumed name. He was accompanied by his stanch friend, the young and wealthy Roger Harlakenden, George Cook, afterwards captain of the Cambridge company, and some sixty others. This company settled at Newtown, and, February 1, 1636, organized a church with much solemnity. The following June, Mr. Hooker and his assistant, Mr. Stone, with their congregation of one hundred people, set out on foot through the wilderness for the Connecticut, a distance of one hundred miles, driving their cattle with them; and, after nearly a fortnight's journeying, reached their destination and founded a second Newtown, the modern Hartford.

A writer, who left America previous to Mr. Hooker's arrival in the country, describes the original Newtown as " one of the neatest and best compacted townes in New England, having many faire structures with many handsome contrived streets. The inhabitants most of them are very rich and well stored with cattell of all sorts. On the other side of the river lieth all their medow and marsh-ground for hay."[2] A later writer, in 1686,[3] affirms that "for handsomness and beauty" it "out-does Boston it self." The town was wealthy, paying, in the spring of 1636, the largest tax in the Colony.[4] From 1634 to 1636, while Dudley and Haynes occupied the governor's chair, the General Courts were held here, and in 1636 additional courts for the trial of cases were established here as well as at several other places. The town was laid out in squares. Its old market-place is the present Winthrop Square, where stood the house of Governor Haynes.[5] Dudley had built, on the west side of Water, now Dunster Street, a house which had incurred the

[1] Johnson's *Wonder-Working Providence in New England*, p. 213.
[2] Wood's *New England's Prospect* (1634), p. 43.
[3] John Dunton's *Letters from New England*, p. 156.
[4] *Records Massachusetts Bay Colony*, vol. i. p. 166.
[5] Holmes's *History of Cambridge*, p. 10, note.

censure of Winthrop as too elegant in its finish for a struggling colony.[1] Near it stood the church, while Bradstreet's house was in what was then Cow Yard Row. An official statement shows that, in 1635, after Shepard's arrival, there were eighty-five houses within the town limits.[2]

These limits were at first very narrow, and the town, in the quaint language of an ancient writer, resembled "a list cut off from the broad-cloath"[3] of Charlestown and Watertown. Very early, however, — it is scarcely possible now to determine just when or how, — it acquired a large territory on the south side of the Charles river. The grant made by the General Court on condition that Mr. Hooker's company should remain, consisted chiefly of the land about Muddy river, the present Brookline, which, on breach of the condition, reverted to Boston. At the General Court, in March, 1636, it was agreed that the bounds of the town should extend eight miles into the country from the meeting-house (on Dunster Street), thus including half of the present town of Lexington.[4] In 1641, 1642, and 1644, the town received very large additional grants, consisting mainly of the territory then called Shawshin. At this period of its greatest size it seems to have extended in a curious irregular line from what was afterwards West Roxbury on the south to the Merrimack river on the north, and to have included the greater part, if not the whole, of Brighton, Newton, Cambridge, Arlington, Lexington, Bedford, Billerica, and probably Tewksbury, and portions of Belmont and Winchester. It should be remembered that the territory near Mount Auburn at this time belonged to Watertown, and that East Cambridge and Cambridgeport, now the most flourishing parts of the city, were then almost uninhabited farms and marshes. The line between Cambridge and Watertown was marked for some distance by a stone wall four feet high, with two gates at the highways, built in accordance with a vote of the proprietors of the town, May 29, 1671.[5]

May 29, 1655, with the consent of Cambridge, the great Shawshin grant became the township of Billerica. August 27, 1679, Cambridge Village, as it was called, was organized as a separate town which later received the name of Newton. The next loss of territory was March 20, 1713, when the Cambridge Farms were set off and organized as Lexington. Little Cambridge and Menotomy (Brighton and Arlington) remained a part of the town until early in the present century.

The year of Mr. Hooker's departure, a theological controversy, originated by Mrs. Anne Hutchinson of Boston, began to create great agitation in the Colony. Mrs. Hutchinson's views were advocated by the Governor, Sir Henry Vane, by John Cotton, and by nearly the whole Boston church. The opposite party was headed by John Wilson, pastor of the church, and Win-

---

[1] Winthrop's *History of New England*, vol. i. p. 73.
[2] Town Records.
[3] *Wonder-Working Providence*, p. 61.
[4] Hudson's *History of Lexington*, pp. 34 and 35, and note.
[5] Town Records.

throp. Party feeling ran high, and at a session of the Court, held at Boston, March, 1637, it was voted, in spite of the Governor, who refused to put the question, that the next General Court, which was to elect officers for the year, should be held in Newtown. The Court met, May 17th, in the open air on the Newtown Common amid great excitement. Mrs. Hutchinson's adherents, we learn from an unfriendly pen,[1] were violent in their speeches, and the two parties well-nigh came to blows. In the midst of the tumult Wilson climbed a tree, and thence addressed the people with marked success.[2] The elections were held. Mrs. Hutchinson's party were entirely defeated, and Winthrop was elected governor. August 30th, a synod, summoned by the ministers with the magistrates' consent for the settlement of the controversy, met in Mr. Shepard's church at Newtown. It included all the ministers, the messengers of the various churches, and the magistrates, and was presided over by Hooker and Bulkeley. This assembly sat twenty-four days, during which the tact and exertions of Governor Winthrop were generally successful in maintaining harmony and good feeling, although some were "so obstreperous that the magistrates were constrained to interpose with their authority,"[3] which resulted in the withdrawal of some of the Boston people. The synod finally agreed in condemning almost unanimously eighty-two opinions, "some blasphemous, others erroneous, and all unsafe;"[4] and also decided some other points of importance. The General Court, at its next session, November, 1637, also held at Newtown, summoned Mrs. Hutchinson into its presence, and after a long examination banished her almost unanimously. It also banished, disfranchised, or disarmed, many of her adherents, and removed the powder and ammunition from Boston, the stronghold of her party, to Newtown and Roxbury.

During these exciting times, the first steps were taken toward the establishment of a college, and Newtown was selected for its site. Here, "at the end of a spacious plain more like a bowling-green than a wilderness,"[5] was built the first college in British America, which, in 1639, took the name of its first benefactor, John Harvard. In May, 1638, the Court gave its sanction to a change of name already made by popular usage,[6] and Newtown became Cambridge, in honor of the great University where its own ministers, Hooker, Stone, and Shepard, and many other leading men in the Colonies, had received their education.

About the beginning of the year 1639, under the auspices of the magistrates and elders, a printing-press, the first in the country north of Mexico, was established at Cambridge. For some time it was under the superintendence of the President, and its profits formed a part of the revenues of

[1] Winthrop's *History of New England*, vol. i. p. 220.
[2] Hutchinson's *History of Massachusetts*, vol. i. p. 62, note.
[3] Hubbard's *History of New England*, p. 302.
[4] Winthrop's *History of New England*, vol. i. p. 238.
[5] *Wonder-Working Providence*, p. 164.
[6] *Records Massachusetts Bay Colony*, vol. i. p. 180.

the college. It was early employed in printing the Bay Psalm Book, and, later, Eliot's Indian Bible.

In 1643, there was a meeting in the college, of all the ministers of the Colony, numbering about fifty, for the purpose of opposing certain incipient tendencies toward Presbyterianism. These distinguished men, during their stay, were boarded at commons for the modest sum of sixpence a meal. Again, in 1645, July 1st, the ministers held a general meeting here for the purpose of revising certain theological works prepared by Hooker and others, and designed to be printed in England.

September 1, 1646, at the instance of the General Court, a memorable synod, called together from all the united colonies to establish a system of church government and discipline, met in Cambridge. After three short sessions, at very long intervals, it finally adjourned, in the summer of 1648, having unanimously adopted the Confession of Faith of the Westminster Assembly, and having framed a "Platform of Church Discipline," which, with little variation, formed the fundamental rule of the Congregational churches for more than a century. An interesting feature of this synod was a sermon preached by John Eliot to the Indians, in their native language, in presence of the whole assembly and the legislature, June 9, 1647. On the 28th of the previous October, at the Indian settlement of Nonantum, then within the limits of Cambridge, on the south side of the river, he had begun with good success his efforts to civilize and Christianize the natives. The remains of the stone walls and ditches with which his early converts surrounded their town, previous to their removal, in 1651, to Natick, were long visible. A few of the Indian youth were educated, and an Indian college was built at Cambridge, but was afterwards devoted to other purposes.

Meanwhile, urged by pecuniary embarrassments, Mr. Shepard's company had been twice on the verge of following the example of their predecessors. In 1640 and 1641, they seriously meditated an emigration to Mattabesett, on the Connecticut,[1] the modern Middletown, and a second scheme of migration, perhaps within the Plymouth limits, induced the General Court, March, 1644, to make them a grant of land on condition of their remaining.[2]

Cambridge seems at this time to have had some commerce with foreign parts, and several of her ships are mentioned by early writers, notably one carrying fourteen guns, which, on a voyage to the Canaries, about the close of the year 1644, fought nearly all day at close quarters, and finally beat off an Irish man-of-war of superior force.[3]

About the year 1650, a woman is said to have suffered death here for the crime of witchcraft, one of the earliest victims to that dreadful popular delusion.[4] Ten years later, in 1660, Elizabeth Horton, a Quaker, went

---

[1] Albro's *Life of Shepard*, pp. 242-245.
[2] Hudson's *History of Lexington*, p. 37. *Records Massachusetts Bay Colony*, vol. ii. p. 62.
[3] Winthrop's *History of New England*, vol. ii. p. 219.
[4] Hutchinson's *History of Massachusetts*, vol. ii. p. 22.

through the streets proclaiming that the Lord was coming with fire and sword to plead with the people.[1] An amusing instance of the paternal system of government adopted by the Puritans, is afforded by the action of the selectmen of Cambridge, February 14, 1676, appointing four persons "to have inspection into families that there be no bye drinking or any misdemeanor whereby sin is committed, and persons from their houses unseasonably."[2]

July 27, 1660, immediately on their arrival in America, Colonels Goffe and Whalley, the regicide judges, took up their abode in Cambridge, where they received a cordial welcome, and remained till February 26th, when they fled to Connecticut. Alarmed by the distant mutterings of the devastating storm of Indian war, which, in 1675, burst on the Colony, the Cambridge militia began the erection of a stockade, for the defence of the town;[3] but Philip's death prevented its completion.

Through the earlier part of the eighteenth century, the history of Cambridge presents little worthy of note. The General Court was several times held here, usually to escape the small-pox prevailing in Boston; once, in 1729, in consequence of a dispute with Governor Burnett. On one of these occasions, in 1764, Harvard Hall, where they sat, was consumed by fire, on the night of January 24th, with the philosophical apparatus and the valuable library of the college, including all but one of the books bequeathed by John Harvard.

In 1740, George Whitefield preached here more than once, addressing himself in the most direct and unsparing manner to the students and tutors. In 1749, a female slave was burned at the usual place of execution in Cambridge, for the crime of poisoning her master.[4]

June 16, 1769, the General Court was adjourned to Cambridge by Governor Bernard, in consequence of the unwillingness of the members to transact business in Boston while the town was held and the very state-house menaced by English troops. The next year, Lieutenant-Governor Hutchinson, in accordance with instructions from England, summoned the General Court to meet at Cambridge, March 15th. A long struggle ensued between the legislature and the executive. The former offered repeated and vigorous but ineffectual remonstrances against the removal of the Court from Boston, and in September, 1770, observed a day of solemn prayer and humiliation, at which the two Cambridge ministers were requested to perform the religious exercises. It was not until June 13, 1772, that the Governor consented that the Court should be adjourned to Boston.

In the year 1761, at the instance of several wealthy gentlemen, an Episcopal church was established in Cambridge, under the charge of the Rev.

[1] Hutchinson's *History of Massachusetts*, vol. i. p. 187.
[2] Town Records.
[3] *Records of Massachusetts Bay Colony*, vol. vi. p. 89.
[4] Drake's *Historic Fields and Mansions of Middlesex*, p. 170.

East Apthorp. He was received in no friendly spirit by the Congregational ministers, and in a few years sought a more agreeable field of labor in England. The breaking out of the war drove his successor, the Rev. Winwood Serjeant, and his congregation of wealthy loyalists, from the town, and the church was closed. In the agitations preceding the Revolution, Cambridge, in spite of these same numerous and influential loyalists, ardently espoused the popular cause. The people "discovered a glorious spirit, like men determined to be free." In 1765, October 14th, they adopted patriotic resolutions against the Stamp Act. In 1770, they tolled their bells on the burial day of the Boston rioters killed by the troops. November 26, 1773, they passed energetic resolutions against the tax on tea, expressing their willingness to join with Boston and other towns, on the shortest notice, to deliver themselves and their posterity from slavery.[1]

September 1, 1774, a military detachment sent by General Gage, seized and carried off a quantity of powder from Charlestown, and two small field-pieces from Cambridge. The news spreading rapidly, roused the neighboring country, and the following day, an excited multitude from the surrounding towns poured into Cambridge, and took possession of the Common. They compelled Judges Danforth and Lee, two of the mandamus councillors recently appointed in violation of the charter, to announce from the court-house steps their resignation of their seats at the council-board, and they exacted pledges of fidelity to the charter from the High Sheriff and County Clerk. At the request of Lieutenant-Governor Oliver, who hastened to Boston to assure General Gage of the respectable and orderly character of the assemblage, no troops were sent out against them, otherwise the Revolution might have had an earlier beginning. In the afternoon, re-enforced by fresh arrivals, they surrounded Oliver's house, three to four thousand strong, a quarter part in arms, and, by violent threats, compelled him to sign a paper resigning his seat as president of the council. After which they peaceably withdrew.[2]

October 17th, the first Provincial Congress, presided over by John Hancock, met by adjournment from Concord, in the First Church, where it continued to hold its sessions till its dissolution, December 10th. Here, too, the Committee of Safety held, apparently, its first meeting, November 2d, as well as many meetings the following year.

The annals of Cambridge for 1775, are a part of our national history, and can here be only briefly referred to. February 1st, the second Provincial Congress met in the church, but on the 16th adjourned to Concord. Cambridge bore its part in the fighting, and the losses of the memorable 19th April, and its selectmen made an ineffectual effort to check the advance of Lord Percy's re-enforcements, by taking up the planks of the Brighton bridge. After the battle, the town became one of the chief rendezvous for

[1] Town Records.
[2] *American Archives*, 4th series, vol. i. pp. 762–769.

the rapidly-gathering patriot forces, and the deserted halls of the college, and houses of the loyalists, and even Christ Church itself, were occupied for military purposes. Here was probably the spot where, early in May, were erected the first of the American fortifications. Here General Artemas

CONGREGATIONAL CHURCH.

Ward, commander-in-chief of the Massachusetts troops, fixed his head-quarters. Here General Washington assumed command of the American army, and here the head-quarters and centre of the army remained during the siege. In the midst of such unwonted scenes of military activity, the eventful year 1776 dawned on the hitherto peaceful town.

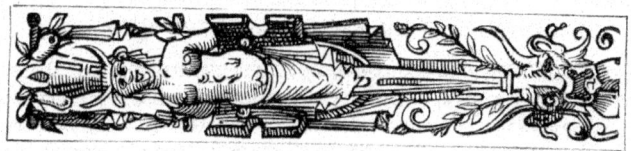

THE INFLUENCE OF CAMBRIDGE IN THE FORMATION OF THE NATION.

BY ANDREW P. PEABODY, D. D.

CAMBRIDGE was the first capital of our infant Republic, the cradle of our nascent liberty, the hearth of our kindling patriotism. Before the 3d of July, 1775, there were tumults, conflicts, bold plans, rash enterprises; but there was no co-ordinating and controlling will, purpose, or authority. On and from that day the Colonies were virtually one people. Before, they had nothing in common but their grievances. They were as yet British provinces, — though wrenching the cords that held them, still undetached, and with no mode of action upon or with one another. By adopting the army and choosing its head they performed their first act, not of alliance, but of organic unity, and became a nation unawares, while they thought themselves still wronged and suppliant dependencies of the British crown. They thus decided the question between a worse than unsuccessful rebellion and revolution.

That the rebellion, as such, would have been an utter failure, is only too certain. The American party in England had on its side eloquence, indeed, and wisdom, but neither numerical force in Parliament, nor the power to mollify ministerial obstinacy, or to penetrate with a sense of right the crass stupidity on the throne. Boston was held by disciplined, thoroughly armed, and well-fed troops, under officers of approved skill and prowess, strongly entrenched and fortified at accessible points, and sustained by a formidable naval force. Hardly one in fifty of the colonial army had had any experience in war, and I doubt whether there was a single man among them, officer or private, who was a soldier by profession. They had come from the farm and the forge, with such arms and equipments as they could bring; they had no bureau of supply, no military chest, no organized commissariat, and their stock of ammunition was so slender that it was ordered by the Provincial Congress that no salute should be fired on the reception of the Commander-in-chief. They were from four different provinces, under as many generals, with sectional jealousies which the common cause could hardly keep at bay; and harmonious counsels could be maintained or expected only and scarcely at moments of imminent peril. At Bunker Hill they had shown both their strength and their weakness, their unsurpassed courage and their poverty of resource. Superior in the conflict, overwhelming the enemy with the shame and disaster of a signal defeat, they had been compelled to yield the ground on which they had won imperishable glory, and to see the heights they had so bravely defended occupied by a hostile battery. They held Boston beleaguered by the prestige of that day, too feeble to press the siege, yet, as they had well proved, too strong to be dislodged and scattered, but by the disintegrating elements in their own unorganized body. These elements were already at work, and the secession of even a single regiment would have been the signal for speedy dissolution and submission to the royal government.

WASHINGTON ELM.

This precarious condition of affairs was beyond the remedial authority of the individual provinces. Massachusetts could choose a general for her own troops, but could not place the forces of New Hampshire, Connecticut, and Rhode Island under his control. Still less could any efficient system of sustenance or armament have been arranged by separate legislatures. A central authority alone could carry forward the resistance so nobly begun. The Continental Congress would in vain have passed patriotic resolutions, protests against tyranny, votes of sympathy; in vain would they have aroused popular indignation and multiplied centres of resistance through the land. The one decisive act in the struggle, the seal of what had been achieved, the presage and pledge of all that should ensue in the coming years, was the taking command of the American army at Cambridge, by Washington.

Cambridge was for obvious geographical reasons the only place where the provincial troops could have their head-quarters, — lying near enough to the enemy to watch and check his movements, yet protected from sudden or insidious attack by the intervention of the then unbridged arm of the sea which separates it from Boston. There was, at the same time, an intrinsic fitness that the opening scenes of the great drama should be enacted here, where so many of the leaders in counsel and arms had learned to loathe oppression and to hold the cause of liberty sacred.

From its earliest days our university had always been on the side of freedom. Its first two presidents were far in advance of their times in their views of the right of the individual man to unrestricted liberty of thought, opinion, speech, and action. Increase Mather, when president, took the lead in the opposition to the tyrannical acts of Andros and Randolph, sailed for England as the unofficial agent of the aggrieved colonists, was appointed to an official agency on the news of the revolution of 1688, bore an important part in the construction of the new provincial charter and in securing its acceptance, and nominated to the royal court the governor, council, and principal officers under it. His successors were of a like spirit, and there is on record no instance in which the college succumbed to usurpation, stooped to sycophancy, or maintained other than an erect position before the emissaries of the royal government. The culture of the students was in great part classical, and in the last century the classics were the text-books of all lovers of freedom. A sceptical criticism had not then cast doubt on any of the stories of ancient heroism, nor had a minute analysis laid bare the excesses and defects of the early republics, whose statesmen and warriors were deemed the peerless models of patriotic virtue, and whose orators thrilled the hearts of their New England readers, as they had the Athenian *demos*, the senate in the capitol, or the dense masses of Roman citizens in the forum.

Almost all the Massachusetts clergy, perhaps the major part of those of New England, had been educated here. The Tories among them were very few, and nearly the whole of their number were ardent patriots. The pulpit then sustained in affairs of public moment the part which is now borne by the daily press; its utterances during the eventful years of our life-struggle had no uncertain sound ; and the champions, deeds of prowess, and war-lyrics of the Hebrew Scriptures gave the frequent key-note to sermon, prayer, and sacred song.

Among the pioneers and guiding spirits of the Revolution, who were graduates of the college, when I have named the Adamses, Otises, Quincys, Warrens, Pickering, Hancock, Trumbull, Ward, Cushing, Bowdoin, Phillips,

I have but given you specimens of the type and temper of those who for many years had gone from Cambridge to fill the foremost places of trust and influence throughout and beyond our Commonwealth. That they carried with them hence their liberal views of government and of the rights of man, we well know in the case of those of whose lives we have the record. Thus we find John Adams, just after graduating here, more than twenty years before the declaration of independence, writing to a friend his anticipations for America, not only of her freedom from European sway, but of her becoming the chief seat of empire for the world. Year after year, on the commencement platform in the old parish church, had successive ranks of earnest young men rehearsed to greedy ears the dream of liberty which they pledged faith and life to realize.

In the successive stages of the conflict of the Colonies with the mother country, the college uniformly committed itself unequivocally on the patriotic side. When the restrictions on the colonial trade called forth warm expressions of resentment, the senior class unanimously resolved to take their degrees in what must then have been exceedingly rude apparel, — homespun and home-made cloth. When tea was proscribed by public sentiment, and some few students persisted in bringing it into commons, the faculty forbade its use, alleging that it was a source of grief and uneasiness to many of the students, and that banishing it was essential to harmony and peace within the college walls. After the day of Lexington and Concord, all four of the then existing college buildings were given up for barracks, and the president's house for officers' quarters. When the Commander-in-chief was expected, this house was designated for his use, with the reservation of a single room for President Langdon's own occupancy. Though the few remaining students were removed to Concord, the President, an ardent patriot, seems to have still resided here, or at least to have spent a large portion of his time near the troops; for we find frequent traces of his presence among them, and on the eve of the battle of Bunker Hill he officiated as their chaplain. In connection with the prevailing spirit of the university, it is worthy of emphatic statement that the Commander-in-chief was the first person who here received the honorary degree of Doctor of Laws.

To Harvard graduates the country was indebted for the choice of the illustrious chieftain. The earliest mention that we can find of Washington's name in this connection is in a letter of James Warren to John Adams bearing date the 7th of May. Adams seems at once to have regarded him as the only man fitted for this momentous service. Though the formal nomination was made by Mr. Johnson of Maryland, Mr. Adams on a previous day first designated Washington as "a gentleman whose skill and experience as an officer, whose independent fortune, great talents, and excellent universal character would command the approbation of all America, and unite the cordial exertions of all the Colonies better than any other person in the Union." There were, however, objections on sectional grounds and personal ambitions that required the most delicate treatment, and it was mainly in consequence of Mr. Adams's strong will, untiring effort, and skilful handling of opposing wishes and claims, that the final ballot was unanimous. On the 5th of June the election was made. It was formally announced to Washington by Hancock, the President of Congress, and was accepted on the spot.

The commander, impressed with the imminence of the crisis, denied himself the sad privilege of a farewell in person to his own household, took leave of his wife in a letter equally brave and tender, and on the 21st commenced his northward journey. Twenty miles from Philadelphia he met a courier with tidings of the battle of Bunker Hill. Eagerly inquiring as to the details of the transaction, and learning the promptness, skill, and cour-

OLD PRESIDENT'S HOUSE.

age that had made the day forever memorable, he exclaimed, " The liberties of the country are safe ! " A deputation from the Provincial Congress met him at Springfield, and volunteer cavalcades gave him honorable attendance from town to town, till, on the 2d of July, he arrived at Watertown, received and returned the congratulatory address of the Congress there assembled, and was then escorted by a company of horse and a goodly body of mounted civilians to the president's house, now known as Wadsworth House. The rapid journey on horseback from Philadelphia to Cambridge, and that in part over rough roads, — an enterprise beyond the easy conception of our time, — must have rendered the brief repose of that midsummer night essential to the prestige of the morrow, when on the first impressions of the hour may have been poised the destiny of the nation.

There were reasons why Washington not only might have been, but would inevitably have been ill received, had he not been made to win men's confidence and love. Several of the officers already on the ground had shown their capacity for great things, and had their respective circles of admirers, who were reluctant to see them superseded by a stranger ; and had not the officers themselves manifested a magnanimity equal to their courage, the camp would have been already distracted by hostile factions. Then, too, the Virginian and New England character, manners, style of speech, modes of living, tastes, aptitudes, had much less in common at that time of infrequent intercourse than half a century later, when, as we well know, apart from political divergence, mere social differences were sufficient to create no little mutual repugnancy. Washington was also well known to be an Episcopalian, and Episcopacy, from the first offensive on Puritan soil, was never more abhorred than now, when its Northern professors, with hardly an exception, were openly hostile to the cause of the people,— when in Cambridge almost every conspicuous dwelling from Fresh Pond to the Inman House in Cambridgeport had been the residence of a refugee royalist member of the English Church.

The morning of the 3d of July witnessed on the Cambridge Common, and at every point of view in and upon the few surrounding houses, such a multitude of men, women, and children as had never been gathered here before, and perhaps never afterwards assembled until its hundredth anniversary was celebrated. Never was the advent or presence of mortal man a more complete and transcendent triumph. Majestic grace and sweet benignity were blended in countenance and mien. He looked at once the hero, patriot, sage. With equal dignity and modesty he received the thunders of acclamation, in which every voice bore part. His first victory, the prestige of which forsook him not for a moment during the weary years that followed, was already gained when under the ancient elm he drew his sword as commander-in-chief. He had conquered thousands of hearts, that remained true to him to their last throb. The wife of John Adams writes of his appearance at that moment, "Those lines of Dryden instantly occurred to me, —

> Mark his majestic fabric! He's a temple
> Sacred by birth, and built by hands divine;
> His soul's the deity that lodges there;
> Nor is the pile unworthy of the God.'"

EXTRACTS FROM THE DIARY OF DOROTHY DUDLEY.

From April 18*th*, 1775, *to July* 19*th*, 1776.

"The Indian's shaft, the Briton's ball,
The sabre's thirsting edge,
The hot shell, shattering in its fall,
The bayonet's rending wedge, —
Here scattered death; yet, seek the spot,
No trace thine eye can see,
No altar, — and they need it not
Who leave their children free!"
O. W. HOLMES.

CAMBRIDGE, *April* 18*th*, 1775. — To-day nine Redcoats stopped at Bradish tavern for dinner and then gallopped on toward Lexington. I wonder what mischief is in the wind now! Mr. Hancock, Mr. Samuel Adams, are staying with Mr. Clark in Lexington, and these officers may be spies in search of them. We are on the alert, knowing that at any moment the war cloud may burst.[1]

April 20*th*. — It has come. The long expected blow has been struck, and by the British arm. How can I nerve myself to write of the horrors of yesterday; but I will do it.

At midnight of Tuesday we were awakened by the ringing of bells and beating of drums and the hurried tread of men arming for battle. The air was filled with cries of frightened women and children. "The regulars are out. To arms!" was the shout which, with lightning speed, went from mouth to mouth. Then we knew that the purposes of General Gage had ripened into deeds, and war was fairly upon us. Our minute-men were ready for action, and as the sun arose set off in the direction of Lexington, where the British troops had gone. For us at home there was the most terrible suspense to be endured. At noon came a body of Redcoats, led by Lord Percy, over the bridge from Boston, to re-enforce the troops which went through our town Tuesday night. It was not till toward evening that our anxiety and suspense could be relieved by any certain news. Then the King's troops were retreating in most ignominious haste before the pursuing militia of Lexington, Concord, and Cambridge.

[1] Though Miss Dudley carefully attributes her interest in public events to "patriotism," the exactness and promptness of her information suggest that some gallant officer gave her intelligence of his movements, and that we owe her details rather to the tender passion than to the love of country. — ED.

As they ran over the road they had so proudly marched over the night before, the slaughter among them was terrible. Several of our brave Cambridge men are killed. Mrs. Hicks sent her eldest boy to look for his

GENERAL JOSEPH WARREN.[1]

father as night came on.[2] He found him lying dead by the roadside, and near him Mr. Moses Richardson and Mr. William Marcy.[3] These three

[1] The face in this portrait is from an engraving after Copley.
[2] John Hicks lived in a house that is still standing on the corner of Winthrop and Dunster streets. It is supposed that he was engaged in the Boston "Tea Party." He was absent from home on that night, and is said to have had tea in his clothing upon his return. — ED.
[3] A monument to these men stands now in the church-yard, near Christ Church. — ED.

were brought home and hastily buried in one common grave in the churchyard. Ah, the sorrows of that night! How near it brought war to our doors, this first burial of victims of British tyranny.[1] It was no time for funeral ceremonies; and as the terrified and sorrowing friends stood around the rude grave in which was put all that was mortal of these brave men, Dr. Warren tried to comfort them with hopeful words. "It will soon be over," he said, "then rightful honors will be paid to these who fell in defence of our country." I cannot forget it. The lurid glare of the torches, the group in the graveyard, the tender but hurried burial without service or even coffins, and Elias Richardson's act of filial love in carefully spreading the cape of his father's overcoat upon the dead man's face, lest the cold earth should fall directly upon it. Dr. Warren himself, they say, had a very narrow escape in the affray. He ran recklessly into it when the British were retreating, and a bullet whizzed past his head, taking off one of the side curls.

April 21st. — Our little town is the seat of war. An army is gathering in our midst in response to the call of the Committee of Safety. Yesterday immediately after the affair at Lexington and Concord, a proclamation to the Colonies was issued, urging them to do all in their power to raise an army. "Our all is at stake. Death and devastation are the certain consequences of delay. Every moment is infinitely precious. An hour lost may deluge your country in blood and entail perpetual slavery upon the few of our posterity that may survive the carnage." But the Colonies have not waited for the call. One spirit animates all — the determination to stand by our country in its hour of need — and the universal cry is Liberty or Death. Volunteers come from all quarters, many with nothing but the clothes on their backs, no money, no provisions. Our houses are thrown open to accommodate as far as possible the great throng of men who have rushed to the cause of liberty. General Ward has taken the chief command and is doing his best to bring order out of this chaos. The Committee of Safety have taken up their quarters at Mr. Hastings's house,[2] and General Ward is also there.

Orders are issued that the college be removed to Concord, and the students are going; the library has already been partly carried to Andover. The college buildings are to be used as barracks for the soldiers. The Common is the rendezvous for military; and a busy scene it is, with its groups of excited minute-men and thousand signs of warlike preparations. A great

---

[1] "With heart and hand they wrought
According to their village light;
'T was for the Future that they fought,
Their rustic faith in what was right.
Upon earth's tragic stage they burst
Unsummoned in the humble sock;
Theirs the fifth act; the curtain first
Rose long ago on Charles's block." — *Lowell.*

[2] Known as the Holmes house. — ED.

many of our townspeople have run away, as this influx of soldiers has come. Tory Row is nearly deserted. The widow of Major Henry Vassall has left her house and sought a place of safety. Colonel Stark has his property in charge. All that cannot be made of use to our army is sent to Boston. The barns will be used to store forage for our cavalry horses. Mr. John Borland has abandoned his home [1] and it is taken by the Committee of Safety. Major Phipps, too,[2] thinks discretion the better part of valor, and has departed. We have but little of the Tory element among us now. The Tories who remain are lukewarm in their principles.

April 24*th*. — Boston is in great distress, the very centre, as it is, of the war; in the hands of a cruel and insolent soldiery, and deprived of its supplies from the surrounding country. We cannot realize how hard a life its poor besieged inhabitants must lead.

April 25*th*. — Good news for Boston sufferers! General Gage has proposed a treaty, as much for his own safety and that of his troops, as from any kindlier motives, and agrees "that upon the inhabitants in general lodging their arms in Faneuil Hall, or any other convenient place, under the care of the selectmen, marked with the names of the respective owners, that all such inhabitants as are inclined may depart from the town, with their families and effects, and those who remain may depend on his protection, and that the arms aforesaid, at a suitable time, will be returned to the owners." He promises that the poor shall be provided for, and asks " that those persons in the country who might incline to move into Boston with their effects, might have liberty to do so without molestation." This proposal is gladly accepted, and the conditions agreed to as just and reasonable.

April 29*th*. — The road to Roxbury is a busy scene, covered, as it is, with an ever lengthening procession of voluntary exiles from Boston, and crowded with loyal subjects of the King, anxious to hide themselves under the protecting care of his Majesty's troops. The Provincial Congress has ordered that provision be made for the Boston exiles in the villages further inland in our Colony, and as many as five thousand are distributed among different hospitable towns. Our army is in a most pitiable condition. There is great and terrible want of powder, muskets, and other necessaries. Congress has offered a reward for the discovery of the best mode of making saltpetre, and all possible efforts are being made to supply the need of clothing, tents, and fire-arms. But I am sure we need have no fears that these raw recruits, as they seem by the side of the disciplined army of his Majesty, will not hold their own and do and dare even to death in defence of our country's liberty. We have had proof of their bravery in our late French war, and their training then and since is not to be despised, as the Redcoats found out to their cost at Lexington and Concord. Our officers, too are men of skill and experience.

[1] The Apthorp House. — ED.
[2] He occupied a large mansion on the present Arrow Street. — ED

Every one knows that "Putnam dares to lead where any dare to follow," and the very name of "Old Put" is a synonym for bravery. Then there is Prescott, who "will never be taken alive" by the enemy, the veteran Stark, and Ward and Pomeroy. With these we have Dr. Warren, a host in himself, the President of our Committee of Safety and also of Congress. He is a wonder to us, so full of energy and enthusiasm, always awake to the necessities of the country, and with such unbounded influence over the soldiers. He it was who despatched the messengers to alarm the sleeping country that memorable night when the British slipped away so secretly on their errand of mischief. While the lanterns hung from the belfry of the North Church in Boston, he said to a friend as he left the town, "Keep up a brave heart; they have begun it. That either party may do. We shall end it; that only one can do." And Warren's name is only one of a list to which Hancock, Church, Devens, Orne, White, Palmer, and Watson belong.

May 20th. — Congress has met in Philadelphia and appointed Mr. Hancock president in place of Mr. Peyton Randolph resigned. Mr. Hancock is very popular, and his vast wealth and influence are all used in the interests of our country. It is said that when the question was discussed in the North End Club of Mechanics, of which he was an active member, how best to drive the British troops from Boston, he cried: "Burn Boston and make John Hancock a beggar if the public good requires it." So we have a patriot at the head of our Congress.

News has come of the capture of Ticonderoga on the 10th of this month by Colonel Ethan Allen and the Green Mountain Boys. It was accomplished without loss of life on either side, by the desperate daring of the hardy mountaineers. They rushed into the fort in the early morning, frightened the garrison by the Indian war-whoop, and were led by the astounded sentry, who made but feeble resistance, to the apartment of the commander. "Come forth instantly or I will sacrifice the whole garrison!" was the thundering command which brought him to the door. "Deliver me the fort instantly," said Allen. "By what authority?" asked the astonished commander. "In the name of the great Jehovah and the Continental Congress!" was the reply. After a short hesitation, he surrendered the fortress, ordering the garrison to parade without arms. This is a valuable acquisition, the fort containing a large number of cannon, stores, and small arms.

Dr. Franklin has arrived from England and is appointed Postmaster-General, also a member of the Committee of Safety and of the Continental Congress. Our councils will gain strength by the presence of this great man. It is such a privilege to have his wisdom and experience employed for the good of our Colonies.

May 23d. — So many of the Boston people have removed from the town that General Gage has become alarmed, thinking that all the patriots will go, and then there will be no restraint upon our troops, to assure the safety of the besieged town. He has broken his promise and forbidden "all merchandise, provisions, and medicine" from passing into the country, and guards are appointed "to examine all trunks, boxes, beds, and everything else to be carried out." Passes, too, are refused now, and many who had procured them are obliged to go without their property, and in several instances families are cruelly divided, and unprotected women and children left with no means of support. Their condition must be wretched indeed!

May 26th. — A re-enforcement from England for the Redcoats, making their army count up to as many as ten thousand men. They are jubilant over this new force, which brings with it Generals Sir William Howe, Clinton, and Burgoyne.

June 13th. — General Gage has issued a proclamation beginning: "Whereas the infatuated multitudes, who have long suffered themselves to be conducted by certain well-known incendiaries and traitors, in a fatal progression of crimes against the constitutional authority of the state, have at length proceeded to avowed rebellion, and the good effects which were expected to arise from the patience and lenity of the King's government have been often frustrated, and are now rendered hopeless, by the influence of the same evil counsels, it only remains for those who are entrusted with the supreme rule, as well for the punishment of the guilty, as the protection of the well affected, to prove that they do not bear the sword in vain." He then goes on to declare martial law and to pronounce those in arms "to be rebels and traitors," and offers pardon to all who will return to loyalty with exception of Samuel Adams and John Hancock, "whose offences are of too flagitious a nature to admit of any other consideration than that of condign punishment." This is an honor many a patriot would gladly risk his life to receive, and only serves to strengthen the opposition and weaken the cord which binds our Colonies to old England.

June 15th. — I heard to-day that when the three British generals with the re-enforcement were sailing into Boston harbor they met a packet coming out, and General Burgoyne asked of the skipper, "What news is there?" The reply was that Boston was surrounded by ten thousand country people. "How many regulars in Boston?" was his next question. "Five thousand." "What!" said the British officer. "Ten thousand peasants keep five thousand King's troops shut up! Well, let *us* get in, and we'll soon find elbow-room."

June 16th. — Colonel Prescott is ordered to be ready with a thousand men this evening to parade on the Common before marching for Charlestown. The men are all farmers, and have no uniform, and no arms except fowling-pieces without bayonets, and carry in horns and pouches their small supply of powder and bullets. Colonel Prescott was dressed in simple blue with three-cornered hat, his tall, commanding figure erect with courage, his eye beaming with enthusiasm. At a signal there was a profound silence, while President Langdon, who is their chaplain *pro. tem.*, offered an earnest and touching prayer for the safety of these brave men, as they go up to battle with the enemy.[1] At nine o'clock they marched, two sergeants carrying dark lanterns in front, and in the rear the tools for throwing up entrenchments. The soldiers are ignorant of the object of their march, and will not be told till they reach its end. Now they have gone and we are left in suspense. What will be the result? We can only echo President Langdon's prayer: "Go with them, O, Our Father, keep them in the hollow of Thy hand, cover them with Thy protecting care, and bring them back to us victorious."

Saturday, June 17th. — We were in great anxiety to know the result of last night's march, when soon after dinner the bells began to ring, the drums beat to arms, and there was great confusion and noise. Adjutants gallopped here and there, crying, "Turn out, turn out; the enemy's all landed at Charlestown." Captain Putnam brought orders from his father to all the Connecticut troops to march immediately to Bunker Hill, to the relief of Colonel Prescott. Captain Chester's company from Wethersfield, which is quartered in Christ Church, and all of Old Put's soldiers in town, marched immediately, and General Warren, who arrived this morning from Watertown, has gone to the field of battle. We can hear the booming of the cannon and see the smoke arising from Charlestown, which the British have set on fire. It is a terrific battle. Our noble men defend their own works gallantly, and will not yield, we know, till the last moment. It is feared that the want of ammunition will force them to retreat before the greater numbers of the enemy.

June 18th. — How can I write of the great and terrible loss which has come to us in the death of our beloved Dr. Warren. Yes, he is killed, pierced through the brain by a British bullet, and left dead on the field. When he was hurrying to the battle, and some one warned him to spare himself, he replied: "Dulce et decorum est pro patria mori." At Bunker Hill, though tendered the command by both Putnam and Prescott, he declined, and took his place with the common soldiers, musket in hand, to do his part in defending the hill. When they were driven to surrender, he was the last to leave the ramparts, and fell bravely fighting. Many others of our brave men are gone, but none so valuable to the country as General Warren. He was appointed major-general only three days ago. Our enemies rejoice at our loss (and well they may), but their victory is a dear one to them, and one they will not care to buy again at the same price. Eleven hundred of their choicest men, including a great many officers, is no small loss, when they receive in exchange only a little hill overlooking Boston. One hundred and forty-five are killed, and three hundred and four wounded among our noble soldiers. It really is wonderful how a small body of undisciplined farmers could stand so long against an army of English regulars. It is owing to the

[1] Authorities do not agree as to the precise position occupied by the President when offering this prayer. — ED.

personal courage and patriotism of every individual soldier, as well as their intrepid leadership; and the great caution exercised in the use of powder, every grain of which served its purpose. Old Put, just before the battle, said: "Powder is scarce, my men, and must not be wasted. Don't fire at the enemy till you see the whites of their eyes — then fire low, aim at their waistbands. You are all marksmen, and can kill a squirrel at a hundred yards. Reserve your fire, and the enemy is destroyed. Aim at the handsome coats — pick out the commanders." Colonel Stark says that "the dead lay as thick as sheep in a fold," on the new-mown hay which covered Bunker Hill. Our brave men have freely given their lives for their country, and convinced the world that we, as a people, are in earnest and ready to die for our cause. Dr. Franklin says: "Americans will fight; England has lost her Colonies forever."

June 19th. — It is feared that the British will follow up their victory and sally forth into the surrounding country, and perhaps attack our camps. General Putnam is busy throwing up entrenchments on Prospect Hill, working day and night, that he may be ready to oppose their progress, while forts and earthworks are building almost by magic around our town.

June 22d. — Our poor wounded men are coming in wagons to the hospitals that are improvised in town. Colonel Phipps's, and Major Henry Vassall's houses, and, further up Tory Row, Lieutenant-Governor Oliver's, and Mr. George Ruggles's, are used for [1] their accommodation. We are doing our best to provide lint and bandages for them. Congress has appointed a day of fasting and prayer, that the battle of Bunker Hill, may, by God's blessing, be followed by great success to our arms. Dr. Appleton preached last Sabbath, a most stirring sermon. Many of the soldiers from camp were at church. And from the hospitals they came too, here and there one whose injuries are light enough to permit him to be out.

June 26th. — Our army at last is to have a commander-in-chief. Our Congress at Philadelphia has appointed Colonel George Washington of Virginia, "General and Commander-in-chief of the Army of the United Colonies, and all the forces now raised or to be raised by them." He is to come immediately to camp to take command, and is now on his way. The Provincial Congress at Watertown has resolved that the president's house, with the exception of one room, reserved by the President for his own use, be taken, cleared, prepared and furnished for the reception of General Washington and General Lee. The appointment of General Washington is very popular. They say he is a man in every way fitted for this position, and his election is unanimous.

July 3d. — General Washington is here. Yesterday he arrived, by way of Watertown, where he was received by Congress with a congratulatory address, and escorted to Cambridge by a troop of light horse. He went immediately to his quarters at the president's house. It was just as we were re-

[1] The Lowell house and the Wells house. — ED.

turning from church, and our curiosity to see the man of whom we have heard so much was satisfied. He is a large man, tall and well-proportioned; his face noble in its suggestion of strength, and dignity, and modesty. Our expectations are more than realized. His appearance is one to inspire confidence and love, and to make us grateful for the possession of such a chief. To-day he formally took command, under one of the grand old elms on the Common. It was a magnificent sight. The majestic figure of the General, mounted upon his horse beneath the wide-spreading branches of the patriarch tree;[1] the multitude thronging the plain around, and the houses filled with interested spectators of the scene, while the air rung with shouts of enthusiastic welcome, as he drew his sword, and thus declared himself Commander-in-chief of the Continental army. He will find his task a hard one, that of making an army out of the rude material gathered from all parts of our Colonies. General Ward, who already commands the troops around Boston, Colonel Charles Lee, who has resigned his commission in the King's service, General Philip Schuyler of New York, and Israel Putnam, "Old Put," are appointed major-generals. These all will surely find their hands full of work, in putting this body of fifteen thousand men into readiness for war, there is so much confusion in camp, so little discipline, and such terrible want of supplies of every kind. And this want must be kept an utter secret from the enemy in Boston. General Washington's staff consists of Major Thomas Mifflin of Philadelphia, first aid-de-camp, Major John Trumbull, son of Governor Trumbull of Connecticut, second aid-de-camp, Colonel Joseph Reed of Philadelphia, private secretary, and Horatio Gates, adjutant-general. Major Trumbull is quite a clever artist, and gained the favor of the Commander-in-chief by a very correct drawing of the enemy's works in Boston. He is a young man of fine appearance and abilities. Major Mifflin is a universal favorite, full of activity and enthusiasm. Colonel Reed is a gentleman of rich culture, and invaluable to Washington as his confidential clerk. General Gates is popular and useful.

July 19th. — General Washington is a most wonderful commander. His personal influence is unbounded. There is something magnetic about him, drawing from others their fullest confidence. He is most conscientious in his discharge of every duty, and is accomplishing miracles among the soldiers.

The army is besieging Boston from all the surrounding country, being stationed in a semicircle from Charlestown to Dorchester, eight or nine miles. Colonel Prescott is entrenched in the woods between Cambridge and Lechmere's Point, and "Old Put" is at Prospect Hill. He has raised the Connecticut flag on the ramparts. On one side the banner has the motto, "An Appeal to Heaven," and on the other side the three vines, the armorial

---

[1] "Under the brave old tree
Our fathers gathered in arms, and swore
They would follow the sign their banners bore,
And fight till the land was free."— *Dr. Holmes.*

bearings of that Colony, with the legend, "Qui Transtulit Sustinet." This was thrown to the air immediately after the reading of the Declaration of Congress, setting forth the reasons for taking up arms against England, and the shouts of the soldiers were so loud as to frighten the enemy on Bunker Hill, who rushed to arms, believing an immediate attack was to be made.

This manifesto declares that "Our cause is just. Our Union is perfect. Our internal resources are great, and, if necessary, foreign assistance is undoubtedly attainable. We gratefully acknowledge as signal instances of divine favor toward us, that His providence would not permit us to be called into this severe controversy, until we were grown up to our present strength, had been previously exercised in warlike operations, and possessed of the means of defending ourselves. With hearts fortified with these animating reflections, we most solemnly, before God and the world, declare, that exerting the utmost energy of those powers which our beneficent Creator hath graciously bestowed upon us, the arms we have been compelled by our enemies to assume, we will, in defiance of every hazard, with unabating firmness and perseverance, employ for the preservation of our liberties, being with one mind resolved to die free men rather than to live slaves."

July 20th. — Fast Day. Services in church and camp. Soldiers are ordered to attend public worship, but to take with them their arms and ammunition, to be ready for battle at a moment's notice. I saw to-day part of a British officer's letter to a friend in England, which failed of its destination. He speaks eloquently of our beautiful Colony, which now is besprinkled with forts and camps, and all the paraphernalia of war: "The country is most beautifully tumbled about in hills and valleys, rocks and woods, interspersed with straggling villages, with here and there a spire peeping over the trees, and the country of the most charming green that delighted eye ever gazed on." Would that he and his countrymen were loath to disturb the quiet beauty of this land by the terrible sights and sounds of war. Our need of ammunition is so great that we are called upon to give up our window weights, to be moulded into bullets; and even the tombs in the old cemetery are robbed of their leaden coats-of-arms, and Christ Church of its metal organ-pipes for the same purpose. The very mention of powder sets every one in a shiver. General Washington sat for a full half hour without speaking, when, in the general council, upon his first arrival, he was told of the great want of that death-dealing substance. But, in spite of its being so ill-prepared for contest, General Washington acknowledges that there is good material in the army, made up as it is "of a great number of men, able-bodied, active, zealous in the cause, and of unquestionable courage." General Washington himself has thrown up the first sod preparatory to building a fort near the river; and the swamps and marshes are dotted with laborers whose whole heart is in their work. The Soden Farm and the pine banks and oyster banks are not to be without redoubts. This matter of entrenchments absorbs the time and thoughts of every one.

July 25th. — A company of riflemen, commanded by Captain Thompson, has joined our army, — a most singular body of men, dressed in Indian costume, with brown linen hunting-jackets confined by wampum belt, leggings and moccasins elaborately trimmed with beads, and a simple round hat. Each carries a tomahawk or knife stuck in his belt, and his own unerring rifle which he brought from his home in the backwoods. They have all come a distance of four hundred, and some as many as seven hundred miles. They are strong, muscular men, looking equal to any hardships; and, from what we hear of their characteristics, we may be sure they will create havoc among the Redcoats. Since their early boyhood they have been trained marksmen, having been punished every time they failed to hit their game in the head.

August 1st. — There is a young man in camp whom I have noticed again and again as he passes the house. He is striking in appearance, though quite small and boyish. His eyes are piercing in their brightness, and there is something winning in his manner. His name is Aaron Burr, a son of Rev. Aaron Burr, formerly President of Princeton College, N. J., and grandson of Rev. Jonathan Edwards. Things are very quiet now in both armies. The enemy is closely hemmed in on all sides by the redoubts thrown up by our troops. With so little ammunition it is impossible to make an attack, or even to answer the volleys from their guns. The other day a shell from Copp's Hill struck very near the president's house, though no harm was done, through the heroism of a soldier who risked his life in stamping upon the still burning fuse. General Washington has desired Colonel John Vassall's house to be made ready for him, and will remove there as soon as possible. Congress has adjourned for five weeks.

[LETTER FROM DOROTHY DUDLEY TO MISS ESTHER LIVINGSTONE OF PHILADELPHIA.[1]]

CAMBRIDGE, *Aug.* 30, 1775.

MY DEAREST ESTHER, — I have an opportunity to send you a letter by a messenger who goes to Philadelphia to-morrow, and hasten to improve it, since I have written so little during the terrible months that have passed. Let me give you a hasty sketch of our Cambridge life since the day when American blood was shed by British troops on Lexington Common. Of course it is all familiar to you through the public prints, — the hanging of the lantern from the belfry tower; the midnight cry which roused every one from sleep; the hurried preparations for the fight; the defeat of the haughty Redcoats with a loss of nearly three hundred from their ranks, which cost our militia nearly one hundred brave men. But you can form no idea of the horrors which fastened themselves upon the poor distressed people of our town. Women, whose husbands had rushed to the affray,

---

[1] The Editor inserts this lively letter at this point because it very pleasantly complements the narrative of the Diary.

The Battle of Bunker Hill.

beside themselves with fright, started off in search of a place of safety, carrying with them their children and such household goods as they gathered together in their haste. Mrs. Dr. Winthrop in the confusion made her way with a number of others toward Fresh Pond, and passed through the battle-ground at Menotomy, where lay the dead bodies of both British and American soldiers. The fugitives were sent to Andover, as it was unsafe for them to return to Cambridge.

The affair that day was the signal for war; and it needed not the appeal for volunteers to bring together hundreds and thousands of brave men on fire with enthusiasm and eager for battle. Our town was deluged with soldiers for the time; and General Heath, the superior officer, was at his wits' end to keep order in the midst of so much coming and going. Many of the men stayed but a few days, and returned to their homes to make preparations for joining the army permanently. General Artemas Ward, the veteran soldier, was put at the head of affairs almost immediately, and the work of levying an army went on rapidly.

You know about Bunker Hill, and the loss of our brave Dr. Warren, who is deeply mourned by all. The memory of that day will live in American hearts, so long as one spark of patriotism burns in our beloved land. Prescott out-did himself, I have heard, in his efforts to spur the men on in defence of their works. He walked back and forth in the redoubt, talking cheerily all the time, and firing the men with his own flaming enthusiasm. General Gage, watching our troops through his glass, inquired who this intrepid officer was. A brother-in-law of Colonel Prescott's told him.

"Will he fight?" he asked.

"Yes, sir; he is an old soldier, and will fight as long as a drop of blood remains in his veins."

"The works must be carried," was the British general's reply.

And they were carried, as you know, though with terrible loss to the British army. Colonel Prescott said after the battle, that he had not done enough to satisfy himself, but we think he has immortalized his name.

Come with me, and I will show you our army, with our matchless chief at its head. Cambridge is a military town, the Common is the parade ground, and Massachusetts, Stoughton, Hollis, and Harvard halls, and Holden Chapel, so lately echoing the tread of students' feet, are occupied as barracks. The beautiful college green is disfigured by earthworks, thrown up in the spring, in anticipation of an attack from the enemy. Christ Church [1] is occupied by soldiers, owing to scarcity of tents. Rev. Mr. Ser-

---

[1] "Our ancient church! its lowly tower,
  Beneath the loftier spire,
Is shadowed when the sunset hour
  Clothes the tall shaft in fire;
It sinks beyond the distant eye,
  Long ere the glittering vane
High wheeling in the western sky,
  Has faded o'er the plain." — *O. W. Holmes.*

The Old Parsonage, built in 1670.

jeant, its rector, has been obliged to leave town, driven away on account of his adherence to the King. Many houses on the Menotomy road,[1] have been given to the army as quarters, and you see military in all corners. Boston is encircled with our troops ; actually hemmed in, though we are weak by reason of the sad want of powder and other necessary supplies. You remember Colonel Vassall's [2] magnificent house on the road to Watertown. It is taken by our government, and is now General Washington's head-quarters. Major Henry Vassall's, on the opposite side of the road,[3] is a hospital for the wounded at Bunker Hill.

Judge Lee, being lukewarm in his Tory principles, and not interfering in politics, is allowed to retain his fine old mansion, the frame of which was brought from the old country, years before the present owner was born. Mr. Jonathan Sewall,[4] you know, has fled, and Captain George Ruggles.[5] The latter's house is filled with wounded soldiers just now, as is also Colonel Phipps's,[6] which you remember. Mr. Ralph Inman has left his estate, and Old Put makes the house his head-quarters, his troops occupying barracks on the grounds. On that terrible 19th of April, when the affray at Lexington had filled the very air with horror, many families, frightened from their homes by the sounds of approaching battle, congregated at Mr. Dana's house on Butler's Hill,[7] and there our good pastor, Dr. Appleton, met his little flock, to comfort and cheer their timid hearts, and lead their thoughts upward to Him whose arm is strong to help in time of need. While engaged in fervent prayer, the cry was heard, " The Redcoats are running," and with thankful haste the patriotic minister said " Amen," and the company dispersed.

You remember Dr. Appleton, with his kindly eyes and benevolent smile. I must tell you an anecdote characteristic of him, in the days when Harvard College harbored roguish students within its walls, in place of its present occupants. The Doctor had a number of hens. Some mischievous boys, thinking to have a feast at his expense, one night made a visit to

[1] Now North Avenue. — Ed.
[2] Now the home of the poet, Longfellow, who says of it : —

" Once, ah, once, within these walls,
One whom memory oft recalls,
The Father of his Country dwelt;
And yonder meadows broad and damp,
The fires of the besieging camp,
Encircled with a burning belt.
Up and down these echoing stairs,
Heavy with the weight of cares,
Sounded his majestic tread ;
Yes, within this very room
Sat he in those hours of gloom,
Weary both in heart and head." — Ed.

[3] The Batchelder house. — Ed.   [4] Mr. John Brewster's house. — Ed.
[5] Wells house. — Ed.   [6] On Arrow Street. — Ed.
[7] Now Dana Hill. — Ed.

his hen-roost. The good Doctor had an inkling of their errand, and stationed himself in the friendly shadow of a tree, to watch and listen. There were two of them — one remained below as sentinel, the other climbed the roost to procure the game. One by one he wrung the necks of the astonished and unresisting fowls, and tossed them to the ground. At last he came to the old rooster, and called down in a whisper: "Say, Jack, here's the old rooster. Shall we take him?" Jack, meanwhile, had been alarmed by a rustling noise behind him, and, turning, discovered his pastor. Without a word he precipitately departed, leaving his friend alone. He, too, had heard the sound, though ignorant of its cause. Again he cautiously spoke: "Quick, Jack, say shall we take him?" A voice in the same tone replied, "Yes, we'll have him. He'll make a nice stew. Hand him down." Down he came, and with him the thief, who, in consternation, recognized, not the partner of his guilt, but the good man whom they were robbing. Not a word was spoken; silently each went his way. In a day or two the whole class, of which these were members, received a cordial invitation to dine with the Rev. Doctor. Every one complied, and they sat down to a dinner fit for a prince. There were roast fowls, and fricasseed fowls, and broiled fowls, with all sorts of tempting dishes, to sharpen the appetite. The Doctor was in his pleasantest mood, and chatted sociably with his guests during the whole of the repast. When they had eaten to their satisfaction, he ordered another dish to be brought on, saying, "You must every one have some of this nice stew, made from the old rooster. It is very good." No one dared refuse, and in no other way was allusion made to the occasion, which furnished this admirable dinner. The Doctor, you may be sure, was not troubled afterwards by thieves.

So you have seen Mrs. Hancock. Is she not charming! One cannot wonder at Madame Lydia Hancock's fondness for her, and resolve to secure the treasure for her nephew. You have heard how carefully she guarded her against the approach of any invader upon Mr. John Hancock's rights.

I visited Lexington, the other day, and trod the ground so lately wet with the blood of our noble minute-men; went into Mr. Clarke's house, where "King" Hancock, and "Citizen" Adams, were lodged that memorable night before the battle, and walked under the tree, which I am told sheltered them during part of that time of terror. I saw the bullet in the wall of the attic chamber where the family were hid at the time, and where Madame Hancock very narrowly escaped death, a ball grazing her cheek as it passed. After the battle Mr. Hancock, who had his coach and four at hand, left the town, accompanied by his Aunt Lydia and Miss Dorothy Quincy,[1] and rode to one of the neighboring villages, and from there by slow stage to Fairfield, Connecticut. Madame Hancock is well acquainted with Mr. Timothy Edwards, a son of Rev. Jonathan Edwards, and at his house they stopped, and John Hancock and Dorothy Quincy were made

[1] This was a niece of the "Dorothy Q.," immortalized in Dr. Holmes's happy poem. — ED.

man and wife. Mr. Edwards has a nephew living with him, whom he has adopted, and treats in all respects as his own son. Aaron Burr is his name. He is a young man of fascinating manners, and many accomplishments. He was much charmed with Miss Quincy, I have heard, and she in turn was not insensible to his attractions, but Madame Hancock kept a jealous eye

SAMUEL ADAMS.[1]

upon them both, and would not allow any advances upon the part of the young man, toward the prize reserved for her nephew. When the knot was tied that made them one, she felt at liberty to breathe. Immediately after the wedding, they set out for Philadelphia, which has been their home ever since.

[1] This portrait is from the one by Copley, now in Faneuil Hall. — ED.

I wish you were with me this delightful summer weather. I sometimes cannot believe that this busy military camp, with its noise and confusion, its drum-beating and parades, its variegated appearance, so in contrast to the quiet look it was wont to wear, can be the same town of Cambridge I remember a year ago. In my walks I frequently meet sad reminders of the reality of the war; sometimes the slow, limping gait, and the dull thud of a crutch, will call my attention; again a tell-tale sling, will speak of the strength gone from an arm once full of energy in the country's service, or an empty sleeve, or weary haggard face, will touch the deepest depths of gratitude and pity.

Old Mrs. Trowbridge, who is, you know, the soul of goodness, is indefatigable in doing for the comfort of the soldiers in the hospitals. I have been with her several times, to carry dainties for their flagging appetites, and to do many little things to ease the pain and weariness that creep into every hour. It is a pleasure to be able to break the monotony of the long days, and sometimes I have taken a book — perhaps Bunyan's good old Allegory, which is ever fresh and full of life — or better, the Bible, the one book which never grows old, and which yields from its inexhaustible well of treasure, something suited to the individual need of every one who seeks to draw therefrom. The brightening look chasing away the cloud which shadowed many a face, has been more than enough to reward me for my little effort. Very glad I am, if I can make the brave men forget themselves in their eager stories of battle and camp-life, before the cruel bullet brought death to their door. Bunker Hill, I have had rehearsed to me, in all the different aspects it wore to those who were sharers in its glory and its loss. And the French War, too, has furnished theme for many tales of adventure and daring courage, from the lips of veterans in the service.

The Widow Vassall's house, which serves as a hospital, I have been oftener to than to others, because of its nearness to my home. This house has a history of its own dating back I don't dare to say how many years, but somewhere in the last century, and was once the residence of good old Governor Belcher. I have heard that Governor Belcher's wife was once on trial for her life in England for the murder of her first husband, Mr. Steele. It seems he had long contemplated suicide, and at last accomplished the deed, shooting himself through the brain with a pistol. Mrs. Steele, seizing the weapon from his hand, was found by a servant of the family standing, it was averred, in a most suspicious attitude. Upon the testimony of this witness she was tried for murder, but acquitted, having been proved entirely innocent of the crime.

Major Henry Vassall, a brother of Colonel John Vassall, died about six years ago and left the house in the hands of his widow. It is a very fine old mansion, showing signs of wealth in its owners, and there are some peculiarities in its style of building. Major Appleton called my attention one day to a large panel in the wall near the fire-place, opening which he stepped into the cavity and shut the door. I found it hard to believe my eyes as I saw him disappear in the wall, but afterwards made assurance doubly sure by peeping into the closet myself and discovered ample space for hiding treasures of any description, and for secreting a fugitive could he find air to keep him alive. The grounds of the Vassall house extend to those of the Brattle estate, which Major Mifflin has just taken as his residence. These grounds are exquisitely laid out, and are really the finest in New England. Many of the convalescent soldiers, able to stroll about in the soft summer air, have found welcome for them to the Brattle grounds in the nodding leaves and grasses and the sweet odors of the flowers and the gentle call of the fountain. The kind Major and his gentle lady, herself delicate in health, both extend warm sympathy and hospitality to our brave soldiers. So you see, my friend, that my life for a time runs in a different current from its wont. Our hands are soldiers' property now; jellies are to be made, lint to be scraped, bandages to be prepared for waiting wounds. Embroidery is laid aside and spinning takes its place. Oh, there is such urgent need for economy! No one, out of the secret, would believe how little ammunition is in the possession of our army. If you will walk with me through the old burying ground I will show you holes in the tombs of our revered ancestors, made by the removal of the leaden coats-of-arms. This, you may be sure, would not be allowed unless necessity required. You know the graves here date back fully a century and a quarter, and count among them those of the first presidents of our college, as well as many who were held in honor in both public and private life. President Charles Chauncy, the second who held the office, died in 1672, and a long Latin inscription testifies to his virtues and his labors. His wife died four years previous, and I have found her epitaph, which I will copy for you.

M^{RS}

CATHARINE CHAUNCY

AGED. LXVI DYED JAN. XXIIII

AN° DOM MDCLXVII —

Upon ye death of ye pious Mother in God
Mrs Katherine Chauncy, deceased. 24. 11. 67.

Here lies enterr'd wth in this Shrine
A spirit meeke, a Soule divine,
Endew'd wth grace & piety,
Excelling in humility :
Preferring Gods commands above
All fine delights, & this Worlds love,
Whilest here she liv'd, she tooke delight
In reading, praying day, & night ;

> In faith she was a Puritan
> Daily from selfe to Christ she ran
> For aid & help, whilest here she staid :
> O This was ye sweet heavenly trade
> Of this renowned matron ! which
> Was to all saints a Pattern rich,
> Most richly fraught wth grace sublime,
> With meekenesse, & wth love divine :
> By hope she live'd, in faith she stood
> Washt from her sins wth X^{ts} own blood :
> Active, & constant she was here,
> In heaven above ye palme she weares ;
> Wth X^t she reignes, in heaven she sings
> Hosannas to her Lord, & King.
>
> * * * * * * * *
> Death was ye key, wch let her out
> * * * * * * *
> Pale gastly death hath sent his shaft
> And hath by Chance nigh broke our heart
> Deaths volleys sound, sad stormes appeare,
> Mourning draws on : Poore Harverd feare,
> Least this sad stroke should be a signe
> Of suddeine future death to thine.
>
> J. B. 24. 11. 67.

There is an element in our camp life not to be overlooked — I mean the negroes, many of them slaves, who, heart and soul, enter into the interests of our country and render valuable service both in tent and field. It was a colored soldier, you know, who shot Major Pitcairn at Bunker Hill. Many of them are scattered through the ranks of the army, and in the hospitals and the camp faithfully fill offices of various kinds. Is it not a curious custom, that of naming the black boys and girls for heathen gods and goddesses ? I often laugh at the dusky Junos and Venuses which hold sway in the kitchen and the Jupiters and Neptunes and Mercuries who in the old days used to guide the rein and flourish the whip in proud consciousness of family dignity, and now that their Tory masters have gone, enlist their powers for the comfort and care of the soldiers.

I shall expect a reply to my letter by your first opportunity for sending. Be sure to write me as fully of your life as I have written of my own. With love in abundance, dearest Esther, I am your very affectionate friend,

DOROTHY DUDLEY.[1]

September 10th. — General Washington is preparing an expedition to march into Canada by way of the Kennebec river, through the wilderness of north-

---

[1] The Editor is never able to read letters of the heroic age of our country without a regret that the art of epistolary correspondence has been suffered to fall into desuetude. The element of a comfortable prolixity seems to be lost in our modern correspondence.

ern Massachusetts. It will include about eleven hundred men under the command of Colonel Benedict Arnold, who they say is "daringly and desperately brave, sanguinely hopeful, of restless activity, and intelligent and enterprising." His object is the conquest of Quebec. This enterprise makes a break in the monotonous life of the soldiers who are panting for active service, and many have gladly offered themselves for the undertaking, calling, as it does for great powers of endurance and unflinching courage. Young Aaron Burr, who has been languishing under the enforced idleness, and really fretted himself into a fever, has jumped at this opening for adventure and joined himself to the band, in spite of the remonstrances of his friends, who think him ill fitted for the exposure. He has been appointed major.

General Richard Montgomery, who distinguished himself in the French war, and is one of the brigadier-generals appointed by Congress, is in command in Canada. He is a very valuable general, trusty, prompt, and brave, and yet retiring, choosing the quiet and seclusion of home to the noise and distractions of the army. His wife is a daughter of Robert R. Livingston of New York, whose father, the aged Robert Livingston, died soon after the battle of Bunker Hill. This venerable man had always been a stanch patriot, and predicted the Revolution. Often he would say to his grandson, "Robert, you will live to see this country independent." The last words of this octogenarian patriot, as he lay calmly awaiting the death angel, were: "What news from Boston?"

Arnold's expedition will join Montgomery, and the united forces do their utmost to conquer the city of Quebec.

October 10th. — General Gage has sailed for England, and left his command with General Sir William Howe, who is very popular with the army. The British are in great distress by reason of the scarcity of fresh meat and vegetables. The country people cannot sell them any provisions, and their naval supplies are nearly cut off by our armed vessels which defend the coast.

October 15th. — Dr. Franklin and others, a "Committee of Conference" from Congress, have come to consult with General Washington about the advisability of enlisting a new army, as the terms of the present one expire in December. There he goes now, the venerable statesman, philosopher, and sage, walking with our honored chief, whose tall, commanding figure towers above that of his companion. The countenances of both beam with benevolence and modesty and good sense, and show evidence of deep and anxious thought. Dr. Franklin's gray eyes are spectacled, and his whole appearance speaks of wisdom in life's affairs.

Great excitement is occasioned by the discovery of a secret correspondence which Dr. Benjamin Church has been carrying on with the enemy. Dr. Church has had the highest confidence of all, as a member of our vigilance committee, and was specially recommended to General Washington on his arrival in camp as a trustworthy and valuable man and one deputed to meet the Commander-in-chief and escort him from Springfield to Cambridge. To think of his being at heart a Tory all the time! I have a letter of his which was intercepted and never reached its destination. No date, but written apparently soon after the battle of Bunker Hill.

"I hope this will reach you. Three attempts have I made without success in effecting. The last the man was discover'd in attempting his escape, but fortunately my letter was sewed in the waist-band of his breeches. He was confined a few days, during which time you may guess my feelings; but a little art and a little cash settled the matter. It is a month since my return from Philadelphia. I went by way of Providence to visit mother. The committee for warlike stores made me a formal tender of 12 pieces of cannon, 18 and 24 pounders, they having took a previous resolution to make the offer to Gen. Ward. To make a merit of my service I sent them down, and when they received them they sent them to Stoughton to be out of danger, even though they had formed the resolution as I before hinted of fortifying Bunker's Hill, which with the cowardice of the clumsy Col. Gerrish & Col. Seaman was the *lucky* occasion of their defeat. This affair happened before my return from Philadelphia. We lost 165 killed, and since dead of their wounds. 120 now lie wounded — the chief will recover. They boast you have 1400 killed and wounded in that action. You say the Rebels lost 1500 I suppose with equal truth. The people of Connecticut are raving in the cause of liberty. A number from that colony, from the town of Stamford, robbed the King's stores at New York, with some small assistance the New Yorkers lent them. These were growing very turbulent. I counted 200 cannon from 24 to 3 pds. at King's bridge, which the committee had secured for the use of the Colonies. The Jersies are not a whit behind them in Connecticut in zeal. The Philadelphians exceed them both. I saw 1200 men in review there by Genrl Lee, consisting of Quakers and other inhabitants in uniform, with 1000 riflemen and 40 horse, who together made a most warlike appearance. I mingled frequently & freely with the members of the Continental Congress. They were united and determined in opposition and appeared assured of success. Now to come home, the opposition has become formidable. 1800 men, brave & determined, with Washington and Lee at their head, are no contemptible enemy. Adjutant General Gates is indefatigable in arranging the army. Provisions are very plenty, clothes are manufacturing in almost every town for the soldiers, 20 tons of powder lately arrived at Philadelphia, Connecticut, and Providence, upwards of 20 tons are now in camp. Salt petre is made in every colony, powder mills are erected and constantly employed in New York and Philadelphia. Volunteers of the first fortunes are daily flocking to the camp, 1000 riflemen in 2 or 3 days. Recruits are now levying to augment the army to 22000 men. 10,000 militia are appointed in this Government to appear on the first summons. The bills of all the colonies circulate freely and are readily exchanged for cash. Add to this that unless some plan of accommodation takes place immediately, their harbours will swarm with privateers. An army will be raised in the middle colonies to take possession of Canada. For the sake of the miserable convulsed empire solicit peace — repeal the acts or Britain is undone. This advice is the result of a warm affection to my King and to the realm. Remember I never deceived you. — Every article here sent you is sacredly true. — The papers will announce to you that I am again a member for Boston. You will there see our motley council. A general arrangement of officers will take place, except the chief which will be suspended but for a little while to see what part Great Britain takes in consequence of the late Continental petition. A view to Independence grows more and more general. Should Britain declare war against the Colonies they are lost forever. Should Spain declare war against England, the colonies will declare a neutrality which will doubtless produce an offensive and defensive league between them ; for God's sake prevent it by a speedy accommodation.

"Writing this employed a day. I have been to Salem to reconnoitre, but could not escape the geese in the Capitol. Tomorrow I set out for Newport on purpose to send you this. I write you fully, it being scarcely possible to prevent discovery. I am out of place here by choice, therefore out of pay & am determined to be so unless something is offered in my way. I wish you would contrive to write me largely in cyphers — by way of Newport, addressed to Tom Richards, merchant, enclosed in a cover to me, intimating that I am a perfect stranger to you, but being recommended to you as a gentleman of Honor you took the liberty to enclose that letter, entreating me to deliver it, as directed, the person, as you are informed, living at Cambridge ! Sign some fictitious name. — This you may send to some confidential friend at Newport to be delivered to me at Watertown. Make use of every precaution or I *perish*. B. CHURCH."

October 17*th*. — The committee have taken this matter of Dr. Church's treachery in hand but are undecided about the best course to pursue. The traitor is under arrest and his papers seized. At present he is imprisoned in Widow Vassall's house, which has been his residence since his appointment as director-general of the hospital.[1] I caught a glimpse of his face at the second story window to-day as I passed. I wonder how he can look out upon the exquisite beauty of the landscape, bustling with military life, all quivering with intense patriotism as it is, and not feel a conscience twinge at his own despicable conduct.

October 24*th*. — Dr. Jeremy Belknap of Boston is in town, and preached for us last Sunday. His sermon was earnest and full of patriotism, and his

---

[1] This confirms the statement in the account of the Batchelder House on p. 101. — ED.

prayers as well. He prayed for the King, I noticed, though it is becoming common to omit that petition, for the thought of separation from England grows more popular every day. The delegates from Congress have many matters to discuss with the Commander-in-chief — one is the expediency of making an attack upon Boston. Several of the committee wish to see Boston burned to the ground, but General Lee says it will be impossible to burn it unless men laden with bundles of straw enter the town and proceed to set fires in all corners. He thinks that a bombardment would not have the desired effect. It is decided to form a new army with longer enlistments than those of the present one, and the work will begin immediately. The Committee of Conference held its session at the head-quarters of General Washington, and General Greene, who was present the first evening of their arrival, says, in allusion to that great man, Dr. Franklin, whom he viewed with silent admiration during the whole evening : " Attention watched his lips and conviction closed his periods."

November 7th. — Dr. Church has had his trial at last. Who could but pity him while they condemned, as with military escort and the music of fife and drum, he was taken from his improvised prison and carried to the Watertown meeting-house, there to be expelled from his seat in Congress and publicly branded as a traitor ? The General Court resolved that he be sent to Norwich, Connecticut, and confined in jail, "without the use of pen, ink, or paper, and that no person be allowed to converse with him, except in the the presence and hearing of a magistrate of the town or the sheriff of the county where he is confined, and in the English language." What with the disgrace and the discomforts of his prison life, I wonder if he does not believe in his inmost heart that the way of transgressors is hard !

November 12th. — Recruiting orders are given out and it is hoped that an army will be raised rapidly. Another element is added to the noise of camp life — the sound of carpenters' tools, the hammering and sawing and planing preparatory to building winter barracks for the accommodation of the soldiers. There was a skirmish a few days ago at Lechmere's Point, which is an island when the water is at high tide. The cattle which graze upon the salt marshes there were a prize the Redcoats coveted, half-starved as they are, and one worth the risk of a fight to procure. So about four hundred men in a number of boats left Boston and landed at the Point, killed one sentinel and took the other prisoner, and succeeded in carrying off ten cows. The alarm was given and cannon from Prospect Hill were fired upon them, sinking one of their boats and killing two men. A regiment of riflemen under Colonel Thompson marched immediately, and to reach the Point were obliged to ford the river, which was up to their necks, and fired upon the marauders, who made their escape as fast as possible. Two of our men were dangerously wounded. Colonel Thompson behaved with much heroism, and was publicly thanked by the Commander-in-chief for the part played by himself and his brave men. Major Mifflin was there, and I have heard "flew about as if he would raise the whole army." General Washington looks upon this affair as the beginning of a general attack upon our works.

November 15th. — The new army is to be in uniform, and the following order has gone forth : " October 28th. It is recommended to the non-commissioned officers and soldiers, whose pay will be drawn in consequence of last Thursday's orders (especially to those whose attachment to the glorious cause in which they are engaged, and which will induce them to continue in the service another year), to lay out their money in shirts, shoes, stockings, and a good pair of leather breeches, and not in coats and waistcoats, as it is intended that the new army shall be clothed in uniform. To effect which, the Congress will lay in goods upon the best terms they can be bought anywhere for ready money, and will sell them to the soldiers without any profit; by which means, a uniform coat and waistcoat will come

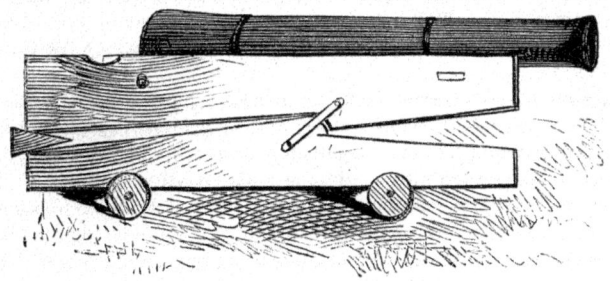

CANNON USED BEFORE BOSTON.

cheaper to them than any other clothing of the like kind can be bought. A number of tailors will be immediately set to work to make regimentals for those brave men who are willing at all hazards to defend their invaluable rights and privileges."

November 28th. — Works have gone up on Cobble Hill,[1] under the direction of General Putnam, and General Heath without any annoyance from the Redcoats. I see by the papers that this redoubt is called "the most perfect piece of fortification that the American army has constructed during the present campaign, and on the day of its completion was named Putnam's impregnable fortress." Washington thinks that this inactivity on the part of General Howe is not without a meaning, that he is planning some grand attack upon our lines, and accordingly batteries are going up in various places to command the important points.

November 30th. — Our vessels at sea have been carrying on war with British ships, and one of ours, the *Washington*, has been captured by the *Fowey*, man-of-war. But success has attended our navy more than once, and to-day has come news of a grand capture — that of the British ordnance

[1] Now the site of the McLean Asylum, Somerville. — ED.

brig *Nancy*, by Captain Manly, commander of the *Lee*. She is indeed a prize, containing a complete assortment of military stores — 2,000 muskets, 100,000 flints, 30,000 round shot, for one, six, and twelve-pounders ; over thirty tons of musket shot, eleven mortar beds, and a thirteen-inch brass mortar weighing 2,700 pounds. So great a loss as this the Commander-in-chief thinks will not be lightly allowed to come to the British arms, and fearing an effort will be made to recover the ship, has immediately ordered four companies to Cape Ann to protect the stores, while all possible haste is used to remove them to a place of safety. One of the officers says that when news of the capture came to the soldiers, '' such universal joy ran through the whole camp as if each grasped victory in his hand ; to crown the glorious scene, there intervened one truly ludicrous, which was Old Put, mounted on a large mortar which was fixed in its bed for the occasion, standing parson to christen, while god-father Mifflin gave it the name of Congress. The huzzas on the occasion, I dare say, were heard through all the territories of our most gracious sovereign in this Province."

December 1st. — Winter is fairly upon us. Snow several inches deep. Mrs. John Adams is in town. I met her at Mrs. Mifflin's last evening. Mrs. Adams is a charming woman, combining ease and grace of manner, and sweetness of temper, with great strength and decision of character. I have the warmest admiration for her. Had a delightful evening. Major Mifflin is very agreeable, and his lady accomplished and winning. The host bustled about on hospitable thoughts intent, making every one at his ease. It seems he was once a Quaker, but was expelled from that peaceable sect when he asserted his determination to arm himself in his country's service. He is an admirable soldier, they say, though so small in stature, and has wonderful influence over his subordinates. General Lee was there. He made a good deal of sport for the ladies by telling stories of Hobgoblin Hall, as he delights to call his quarters at Mr. Isaac Royall's house in Medford, which is truly a magnificent mansion.[1] Colonel Royall has run away, having been terribly frightened at the prospect of war, and having no decided principles, either rebel or loyal ; and is in danger of the one thing he dreaded most of all — confiscation. The house, built by his father in most substantial style, is surrounded by fruit trees of many varieties, and a profusion of shrubbery, and is shut in from the road by a brick wall. General Lee's imagination called up shadowy shapes to answer to his tread through its halls and corridors ; hence the name. The General is a most singular man, very unprepossessing in appearance, tall and thin, with large features, eyes that are never at rest, and a certain air of carelessness, as if he gave not a thought to his dress or manner of life. He has a great fondness for dogs, and is rarely seen without one or more. Last night, " Mr. Spada," a large, shaggy, bearish-looking animal, was with him, and was the source of

[1] This house is still extant in Medford. — ED.

some annoyance as well as amusement to the guests. He insisted upon the dog's presenting his paw to Mrs. Adams, who, as a stranger, was entitled to every mark of attention. "Love me, love my dog," this whimsical man might well say to his friends. He has lived among the Indians long enough to acquire their confidence, and be honored by appointment as chief, and in their expressive way they called him from his passionate nature, "Boiling Water." He has travelled through Europe, and has lost two fingers in a personal encounter in Italy. His courage is undoubted, and his military abilities highly estimated by the Commander-in-chief and his fellow generals. He speaks and writes several languages, fluently, and Mrs. Adams says with truth, "the elegance of his pen far exceeds that of his person." Dr. Morgan, successor to the traitor Church as director-general of the hospital, lives with Major Mifflin in this fine old mansion, which surpasses all others in Cambridge in the beauty of its grounds. Brattle's Mall is a place of wonderful attraction, moonlight evenings in summer. The graceful play of the shadows upon the velvety lawns and well-kept paths, the murmuring hum of the river, the glad rush of the ice-cold water as it bursts from its prison in the marble grotto — all these are so many magnets, each drawing to the Brattle grounds a goodly number of pleasure-seekers. Now, the promenade is wrapt in a soft white dress, which clothes all nature — and dazzling in its purity, hides beneath its veil of charity all the blemishes of our mother earth.

December 9th. — There has been trouble in camp, and some crimes perpetrated of so flagrant a nature as to call for severe punishment. Several of the criminals have been sent to the famous Newgate prison, in Simsbury, Connecticut, once worked as copper mines and now given up for the confinement of the most atrocious villains. I have a copy of the letter Washington sent with the prisoners to the Committee of Safety at Simsbury: —

"CAMBRIDGE, *Dec. 7th,* 1775.

"GENTLEMEN: The prisoners which will be delivered you with this, having been tried by a court martial, and deemed to be such flagrant and atrocious villains, that they cannot by any means be set at large, or confined in any place near this camp, were sentenced to Simsbury, in Connecticut. You will therefore be pleased to have them secured in your jail, or in such other manner as to you shall seem necessary, so that they cannot possibly make their escape. The charges of their imprisonment will be at the Continental expense.   I am, &c.

"GEORGE WASHINGTON."

I saw the prisoners, as under a strong guard they left the court-house after their condemnation to that horrible place. The reports of that underground dungeon are enough to make one shudder. Chained to the damp ground, far below the upper world, out of reach of the sun's rays or a breath of pure air, how can it be possible for life to go on? Surely only the most hardened wretches are entitled to such a fate!

December 11th. — Mrs. Washington, our general's lady, has arrived, and with her many ladies of the families of our officers. She has had a long, tedious journey from Mount Vernon, with bad roads and trying weather, and has come by short stages, stopping often to rest and change horses. She has gone directly to her husband's head-quarters. Mr. Curtis, her son, accompanied her, with his wife.

December 12th. — Our army is in great distress for want of firewood and hay, and a call from the Assembly has gone forth to all the towns within twenty miles of Boston, to supply these articles, each according to its ability. The work on the barracks is completed, and the soldiers are occupying them. As far as possible, they are made comfortable and easy. Christ Church is vacated. Our army daily looks for an attack from the Redcoats, and Washington says he is "unable, upon any principle whatever, to account for their silence, unless it be to lull us into a fatal security." But instead, it has only increased our vigilance, and every possible avenue by which they might approach our lines is guarded. Captain Manly, the brave commander of the *Lee*, has drawn to himself well-earned praise by his skilful manœuvres in the seas. Several vessels with British cargoes have surrendered to his arms. An officer writes that one contained a vast number of letters, and "what is really extraordinary, not one that does not breathe enmity, death, and destruction to this fair land."

December 15th. — I have to-day taken a sad stroll with dear old Mr. Wadsworth[1] about the college grounds. I say it was "sad," because so it seemed, to see the buildings dedicated to education used as barracks, and the once white snow on the ground about them covered with the unsightly rubbish that always abounds where many soldiers remain long. My dear old friend mourned too as we walked from one building to another, and talked constantly about old times at Harvard, and of the traditions he received years ago from Mrs. Wadsworth's father, Mr. Walter Mildmay. Though the college is so old — it is a hundred and thirty-nine years old — the memory of these two men goes back to its beginning. Walter Mildmay knew and often talked with the Rev. Benjamin Woodbridge, whom Cotton Mather called "a star of the first magnitude," and the leader of the whole company of the graduates of the college. He was graduated in the class of 1642, with that George Downing who went to England, became a confidential member of the staff of Oliver Cromwell, and as his minister to Holland rendered such valuable aid to the cause of the Commonwealth. Downing was described by the poet Milton as "a person of eminent Quality." This walk has so much excited my aged friend that he can scarcely talk of anything but the colleges and their history. It is all my gain, for I have learned

---

[1] This "Mr. Wadsworth" cannot be identified. He was evidently not a graduate of Harvard, for none of the three bearing the name were living in 1775. — ED.

many things that I never knew before. Some of these I shall now write down, lest I forget them. It seems that on the 28th of October, 1636, "the General Court of Massachusetts Bay in New England" voted to appropriate £400 to establish a "schoole or colledge," which was the beginning of Harvard.[1] It did not have a local habitation, however, until after November of the following year, at which time Mr. Dudley (I believe he was one of my ancestors), Mr. Winthrop, Mr. Cotton, Mr. Shepard, and others, took "order for a colledge at Newetowne," as the old records say. In May, 1638,[2] the name of the town was changed to Cambridge, and in the following March the present name was given to the college, in honor of the Rev. John Harvard, a godly gentleman and lover of learning, who had been stirred up to give one half of his estate and all of his library to it. At first it was little less than a boarding-school, and was conducted by one Nathaniel Eaton, a person of most disreputable memory. In September, 1639, Eaton was discharged, and fined by the General Court for "cruell & barbaros beating of Mr. Natha: Briscoe, & for other neglecting & misvseing of his schollers." Eaton fled to "Pascataquack," and afterwards to Virginia, with a thousand pounds of his creditors' money. Mr. Wadsworth could not conceal his righteous indignation as he spoke of this man. Indeed, Eaton must have been very brutal, for he beat his poor pupils with little mercy, and had a rule that he would not give over correcting until he had subdued the party to his will. Governor Winthrop tells us that on one of these occasions the master used "a cudgel which was a walnut-tree plant big enough to have killed a horse, and a yard in length." But this was not all; for, though the pupils paid him well for their "diet," it was ordinarily nothing but porridge and pudding, and that very homely. They complained also that Mrs. Eaton denied them butter and cheese and beer "betwixt meals," that she forced them to make their own beds at times, and that she offended "Sam Hough," who was, I presume, one of the "schollers," by letting a certain Moor lie in his "sheet and pillow bier."[3] I am sure the "schollers" had hard times when Mr. and Mrs. Eaton taught and dieted them!

Towards the latter end of summer in the next year the learned, reverend, and judicious Mr. Henry Dunster came over, and was pointed out by the Lord, "with his unerring finger," as the one to take the direction of the young institution, now pretty firmly established with funds, as well as in the faith of the people. More money was soon sent from across the sea, for the enterprise was considered past the reach of a poor pilgrim people. Over the college there were twelve overseers, six being magistrates and six ministers; and the students had the advantage of being "under the orthodox and

[1] The Editor fails to find evidence that this money was ever actually paid.
[2] It was May 2d. — ED.
[3] The curious reader will learn much more on this subject if he consult the doings of the General Court, quoted by Mr. Sibley in his *Biographical Sketches of Graduates of Harvard University*, vol. i. pp. 2–6. — ED.

soul-flourishing ministry of Mr. Thomas Shepard,"[1] a fact that is said to have had great influence in deciding the place at which the college was established. In 1641, a class of nine bachelors, who had probably[2] been under instruction for some time previous to the arrival of Mr. Dunster, was graduated. People rejoiced greatly at the progress of these young men in learning and godliness. Some of the rules of the college provided that no one should be admitted that could not understand Tully, or such like classical author *ex tempore*, and make and speak true Latin in verse and prose. They were to understand that the main end of this life is "to know God and Jesus Christ; and therefore to lay Christ in the bottom, as the only foundation of all sound knowledge and learning." "And seeing the Lord only giveth wisdom, let every one seriously set himself by prayer in secret to seek it of Him.'" Further, they were to exercise themselves in reading the Scriptures twice a day. They could not "go abroad to other towns" without permission; and were directed to eschew all profanity of God's Name, Attributes, Word, Ordinances, and Times of Worship. These rules were not ignored; and it is said that on the first Commencement Day "two young men of good quality, lately come out of England," were complained of "for foul misbehaviour, in swearing and ribaldry speeches," were corrected in the college, and sequestered for a time. For the most part, however, the young men came with a purpose, and worked with a will. They suffered privations, and their parents did also. Money was scarce in the Colony then, and the steward's bills were paid with beef, veal, pork, mutton, poultry, grain, malt, eggs, butter, cheese, apples, cider, fuel, candles, cloth, leather, shoes, and sometimes with tobacco, and even the products of the still. President Dunster labored against financial odds for fourteen years, and was at last compelled to resign on account of certain views on baptism that were considered by some to have originated with the Evil One. Mr. Wadsworth says he was never able to see exactly why a college president should have been compelled to resign for such reasons. The Rev. Charles Chauncy was next president; and during his term of office the financial difficulties increased so greatly that the General Court was appealed to for aid for what was called then "the sinking college." Public grants and private munificence, however, did not fail, and the work went on. Mr. Leonard Hoar, of the class of 1650, became president in 1672, and the same year the library was largely increased by a bequest of Theophilus Gale. President Hoar was a sagacious man, and very creditable every way to his *Alma Mater*.[3] In 1685, the Rev. Increase Mather of Boston, of the class of 1656, became president, and held the office sixteen years. Old Mr. Wadsworth

---

[1] From this learned divine the name of the Shepard Memorial Church is derived. — ED.

[2] "And who was on the Catalogue
When college was begun?
Two nephews of the president,
And *the* professor's son." — *Dr. Holmes.*

[3] See, on this point, *The Harvard Book*, vol. i. pp. 33, 34. — ED.

tells me of a curious visit made to the college in July, 1680, by two Dutchmen from Friesland. They were Jasper Dankers and Peter Sluyter, who were making a tour in several American colonies, and made the following records in their diary : [1] —

"*9th, Tuesday.* — We started out to go to Cambridge, lying to the N. E. of Boston, in order to see their college and printing-office. We left abt. six o'k in the morning, and were set across the river at Charlestown. . . . We reached Cambridge abt. 8 o'k. It is not a large village, and the houses stand very much apart. The college building is the most conspicuous among them. We went to it expecting to see something curious, as it is the only college or would-be academy of the Protestants in all America ; but we found ourselves mistaken. In approaching the house, we neither heard nor saw anything mentionable ; but going to the other side of the building we heard noise enough in an upper room to lead my comrade to suppose they were engaged in disputation. We entered and went upstairs, where a person met us and requested us to walk in, which we did. We found there eight or ten young fellows sitting around smoking tobacco, with the smoke of which the room was so full that you could hardly see ; and the whole house smelt so strong of it, that when I was going upstairs I said, ' This is certainly a tavern.' [2] We excused ourselves that we could speak English only a little, but understood Dutch or French, which they did not. However, we spake as well as we could. We inquired how many professors there were, and they replied not one, that there was no money to support one. We asked how many students there were. They said at first thirty, and then came down to twenty. I afterwards understood there are probably not ten. They could hardly speak a word of Latin, so that my comrade could not converse with them. They took us to the library, where there was nothing particular. We looked over it a little. They presented us with a glass of wine. This is all we ascertained there. The minister of the place goes there morning and evening to make prayer, and has charge over them. The students have tutors or masters. Our visit was soon over."

This account shows that the rules about the use of tobacco and the study of Latin were not always observed, and also that the students in those days were not above having a little fun at the expense of innocent strangers. Increase Mather was an absentee from Cambridge, with the exception of three months and a week, and appears to have considered his collegiate duties of much less importance than those he was called to render the state, and the people of the North Street Church, Boston. Meanwhile, the stu-

[1] This record is to be found also in the *Memoirs of the Long Island Historical Society*, vol. i. — ED.

[2] " Dear haunts of lost or scattered friends,
Old Harvard's scholar-factories red,
Where song and smoke and laughter sped
The nights to proctor-haunted ends." — *Lowell.*

dents were well instructed by tutors Brattle and Leverett of the class of 1680. It was during the presidency of Mather, in 1700, that the book of Robert Calef, on the "Wonders of the Invisible World," was burned in the college yard. The next year Samuel Willard was appointed acting president. He was followed by John Leverett, Benjamin Wadsworth, Edward Holyoke, Samuel Locke, and, a year ago last October, by the Reverend Samuel Langdon, our present earnest, learned, and patriotic president. May he long hold the office! Massachusetts Hall was built in 1720, when Mr. Leverett was president. In 1725, the college faculty was organized. It seems that discipline had grown loose, for, two years before, there were reports that the students were some of them guilty of "stealing, lying, swearing, idleness, picking of locks, and too frequent use of strong drink." These practices were found difficult to be entirely abolished.

In January, 1764, — it seems as if the terrible event were but yesterday, — the college met with its great loss in the burning of Harvard Hall, in which the General Court was sitting. The members were very active in their efforts to save the building; but it went, and with it the library of some six thousand volumes, the gift of Mr. John Harvard, Dr. Lightfoot, Bishop Berkeley, and others; the portraits and curiosities, the apparatus given by Mr. Hollis, and many other articles that can never be restored. This disaster was the occasion of a great display of good feeling, and many gifts of books, apparatus, and furniture were promptly made to the college by friends in America and England. Soon, however, the relations between the Colony and the mother country changed; and, as a token of their feelings, the senior class voted to take their degrees in homespun clothes. Their patriotism was loudly applauded; and they seem to have been led by this fact, and by the atmosphere of rebellion about them, to disobey a rule of the Faculty that was of small importance. I forget what Mr. Wadsworth says it was.[1]

In 1769, the General Court met in the college chapel, and before proceeding to business listened to an impassioned address from Mr. James Otis, of the class of 1743. In 1770, the General Court met again in Cambridge, — but I must stop. My interest in the whole subject of the relations of the college to our present terrible struggle has carried me on and on, until I am surprised at the number of pages I have devoted to it. I hope the record may prove of value to me at some future time, when the matter is less fresh in my memory.

December 18th. — Mrs. Washington was at church yesterday with the General. She is a fine-looking lady, with regular features, dark chestnut hair and hazel eyes, and a certain gravity in her carriage which becomes her position. She was a widow when General Washington married her, rich and attractive, and he was taken captive at first sight. They say General and

---

[1] The rule had reference to excuses for absence from the college exercises. See *The Harvard Book*, vol. i. p. 42. — ED.

Mrs. Gates came with them, and occupied a pew near. Dr. Appleton prayed most earnestly for our country and its defenders, alluding pointedly and affectionately to the chief officer of the army. For some time it has not been customary to pray for the King. Independence is much thought and talked of, and any sign of allegiance to the mother country is very offensive. Mrs. Washington has expressed a wish that Christ Church may be put in readiness for services, and orders have gone forth to that effect.

January 1, 1776. — Yesterday service was held in Christ Church. I was invited to be present. Colonel William Palfrey, at request of Mrs. Washington, read the service and made a prayer of a form different from that commonly used for the King. " O Lord, our Heavenly Father, high and mighty, King of Kings and Lord of Lords, who hast made of one blood all the nations upon earth, and whose common bounty is liberally bestowed upon thy unworthy creatures ; most heartily we beseech Thee to look down with mercy upon his Majesty, George the Third. Open his eyes and enlighten his understanding, that he may pursue the true interest of the people over whom Thou in Thy Providence hast placed him. Remove far from him all wicked, corrupt men, and evil counsellors, that his throne may be established in justice and righteousness ; and so replenish him with the grace of thy Holy Spirit, that he may incline to Thy will and walk in Thy way. Have pity, O most merciful Father, upon the distresses of the inhabitants of this Western world. To that end we humbly pray Thee to bless the Continental Congress. Preside over their councils, and may they be led to such measures as may tend to Thy glory, to the advancement of true religion, and to the happiness and prosperity of Thy people. We also pray Thee to bless our provincial assemblies, magistrates, and all in subordinate places of power and trust. Be with Thy servant, the Commander-in-chief of the American forces. Afford him Thy presence in all his undertakings ; strengthen him that he may vanquish and overcome all his enemies ; and grant that we may in due time be restored to the enjoyment of those inestimable blessings we have been deprived of by the devices of cruel and bloodthirsty men, for the sake of Thy Son, Jesus Christ our Lord. Amen."

General and Mrs. Washington, Mrs. Gates, Mrs. Morgan, Mrs. Mifflin, Mrs. Curtis, and many others, including officers, were present. The General is loyal to his church as to his country, though he has identified himself with our parish during his residence among us. There was something grand and yet incongruous in the service in this church, which has so lately sheltered the rollicking soldiers. Doors shattered and windows broken out, organ destroyed, and the elegance and beauty of the building greatly marred. It has been imperfectly repaired at the request of one whom its former aristocratic worshippers hold in supreme contempt as a rebel against his Majesty's most righteous rule. How very different was the scene from that in the days before the war. The General's majestic figure, bent reverently in prayer, as with devout earnestness he entered into the service ; the smallness of the band of worshippers, and the strangeness of the circumstances and the surroundings. There was nothing but the contrast to recall the wealth and fashion which were wont to congregate there. I remember the families as they used to sit in church. First, in front of the chancel were the Temples, who every Sabbath drove from Ten Hills Farm;[1] Mr. Robert Temple and his accomplished wife and lovely daughters. Their estate, which is a very fine one, is on the supposed site of Governor Winthrop's house as early as 1631, and where, it is thought, the little bark, the *Blessing of the Bay*, the first vessel built in American waters, was launched for its first voyage across the ocean. Mr. Temple is a stanch loyalist, and at the beginning of war took passage for England, leaving his family at the Farm under General Ward's protection. The vessel, however, was detained, and he obliged to take up his residence in our camp. Behind the Temples sat the Royalls, relatives of Mrs. Henry Vassall, the Inmans and the Borlands, who owned and occupied the Bishop's Palace, as the magnificent mansion, built by Rev. Mr. Apthorp, opposite the president's house, is called. The house is grand in proportions and architecture, and is fitted in every respect to bear the name which clings to it. It was thought that Mr. Apthorp had an eye to the bishopric when he came to take charge of Christ Church, and put up this house of stately elegance. But whatever his wishes may have been, they were not realized, for he abruptly terminated his ministry in Cambridge after a few years. Among his congregation were the Faneuils, the Lechmeres, the Lees, the Olivers, the Ruggleses, the Phippses, and the Vassalls. Many of these families were connected by relationship. Mrs. Lee, Mrs. Lechmere, and Mrs. Vassall the elder, are sisters of Colonel David Phipps, and daughters of Lieutenant-Governor Spencer Phipps. The "pretty little, dapper man, Colonel Oliver," as Reverend Mr. Serjeant used to call in sport our sometime lieutenant-governor, married a sister of Colonel John Vassall the younger, and Colonel Vassall married his. Mrs. Ruggles and Mrs Borland are aunts of Colonel Vassall's. These families were on intimate terms with one another, and scarcely a day passed that did not bring them together for social pleasures. Judge Jonathan Sewall, who afterwards occupied Judge Richard Lechmere's house, married a daughter of Mr. Edmund Quincy, an elder sister of Mrs. John Hancock. I well remember the train of carriages that rolled up to the church door, bearing the worshippers to the Sabbath service. The inevitable red cloak of Judge Joseph Lee, his badge of office in the King's service, hung in graceful folds around his stately form; the beauty and elegance of the ladies were conspicuous, as silks and brocades rustled at every motion, and India shawls told of wealth and luxury. The ties of blood and friendship were strengthened by those of a common faith, and the treasury of the church was filled by cheerful givers from their abundance. Now everything is changed — all who took such deep interest in the welfare of the church, all the original

---

[1] Ten Hills Farm is within the present limits of Somerville. — ED.

subscribers for the building are gone, with exception of Judge Joseph Lee, who is unmolested on account of his moderate principles, and Mr. John Pigeon, who is a patriot. The very first article of plate this church possessed was a handsome silver christening basin, the gift of Madame Grizzel Apthorp, Dr. East Apthorp's mother, the first year of its existence as a church and of his duties as rector. It is inscribed : —

ECCLESIÆ CHRISTI
CANTABRIGIÆ IN NOVA ANGLIA
ANATHEMA CONSECRAVIT
DNA APTHORP
MDCCLXI.

The communion service, a silver flagon and covered cup, was presented by Governor Thomas Hutchinson through Dr. Caner, rector of King's Chapel, who had received a new service of communion plate from King George III. for the use of the chapel in Boston. This flagon and cup are inscribed with the royal arms and these words : —

THE GIFT OF
K. WILLIAM AND Q. MARY
TO YE REV'D SAMLL MYLES,
FOR YE USE OF
THEIR MAJESTIES CHAPELL IN N. ENGLAND,
MDCXCIV.

January 2d. — Yesterday a union flag was raised on Prospect Hill. It has thirteen stripes of alternate red and white, emblematic of the thirteen united colonies, Massachusetts, Connecticut, Rhode Island, New Hampshire, New York, New Jersey, Pennsylvania, Delaware, Maryland, Virginia, North and South Carolina, and Georgia, and on a blue ground in the corner are the united red and white crosses of St. George and St. Andrew. As it was flung to the breeze and tossed and spread itself in graceful glee, a volley of thirteen guns thundered forth a glad greeting to our national banner. If one can trust the index of patriotism and determination and bravery, unswerving in the face of dreadful discouragements, this our national flag will ere long proudly wave over a free country. There it is now, flaunting defiantly in the very eyes of his Majesty's troops, who are bewildered by the loud huzzas which fill the air. Yesterday was the birthday of our new Continental army. The first hastily organized one has been disbanded ; within gunshot, too, of twenty or thirty British regiments. The supply of fire-arms is so small that the guns of the retiring soldiers were taken from them to do service a second time in the hands of those who now step into their places. This of course occasions dissatisfaction, as many of the men brought their own muskets when they enlisted. But, I am sure, they will submit to the situation pleasantly when they see the necessities of the government. General Howe shows no disposition to leave Boston, nor does General Washington feel secure enough in the strength of his army to attempt to drive him away just yet. One of our officers from General Putnam's division, speaking of the January thaw, expresses the universal want of the soldiers : " The bay is open ; everything thaws here except Old Put. He is still as hard as ever, crying out for powder, powder, — ye gods, give us powder ! " Congress has resolved " That if General Washington and his council of war should be of opinion that a successful attack may be made on the troops in Boston, he do it in any manner he may think expedient, notwithstanding the town and property in it may be destroyed." President Hancock, in communicating this resolve, wrote : " You will notice the resolution relative to an attack upon Boston. This passed after a most serious debate in a committee of the whole house, and the execution was referred to you. May God crown your attempt with success. I most heartily wish it, though individually I may be the greatest sufferer."

January 4th. — His Majesty's " most gracious " speech has been received. It breathes the tenderest compassion for his deluded American subjects. Yet there is an under-current of revenge and threatening of destruction, if continued rebellion is persisted in. It seems that the day of the flag-raising on Prospect Hill, the speech was sent to General Washington from Boston, and the British, hearing the noise of the shouting soldiers, misinterpreted it as a signal of submission to the King, and are daily looking for a formal surrender of our lines. How very different is the case from that of their anticipations ! The colonists are more united than ever in their resistance. They have burnt the speech, and in every way in their power sought to express their indignation. General Greene says : " America must raise an empire of permanent duration, supported upon the grand pillars of truth, freedom, and religion, based upon justice, and defended by her own patriotic sons. From the sincerity of my heart, ready at all times to bleed in my country's cause, I recommend a declaration of independence, and call upon the world, and the great God who governs it, to witness the necessity, propriety, and rectitude thereof." Great Britain is to hire Hessians to crush our rebellious Colonies. All their efforts will but encounter the most spirited opposition, and we firmly believe will result in nothing but disaster to themselves.

HESSIAN FLAG.

January 16th. — How our Boston buildings are desecrated by the British soldiers! Faneuil Hall, which has rung with the eloquence of patriots, is used as a theatre, where ridiculous plays are performed and our army and its commanders turned into sport. Sometimes the playbills are sent to our officers in camp. A few evenings ago, while they were amusing themselves with a performance called "The Blockade of Boston," in which General Washington was represented as an uncouth countryman, dressed shabbily, with large wig and long rusty sword, suddenly a sergeant appeared and cried out, "The Yankees are attacking our works on Bunker Hill." Immediately General Howe gave the order, "Officers to your alarm posts!" and there was a hasty breaking up of the assembly. The alarm was caused by an attempt of our soldiers to burn the remaining houses in Charlestown, — those that had escaped the general conflagration last June, and which are used for fuel by the British. The flames aroused the enemy on Bunker Hill, and there was some firing on both sides, though only one life was lost on the enemy's side. None of our men were hurt.

January 22d. — A most curious delegation of Indians is in town, of the Caghnawaga tribe; come to visit our army and pay their respects to its Commander-in-chief. General Washington treats them with great attention, and will exert himself to make their stay one of enjoyment, that they may go away feeling the greatness and strength of our government, and our friendship toward their nation.

January 24th. — Have been honored by an introduction to several sachems and warriors of the Caghnawaga Indians. Major Mifflin made a large dinner company, to-day, in their honor and I was invited. The Redmen are very courteous in Indian fashion, and the profound bows and scrapes they made to those favored with presentation are truly remarkable. One of the sachems is of English birth, a native of Massachusetts, carried away in infancy by the savages and brought up as one of their own children. Another has French blood in his veins. They go to-morrow, I believe, to Roxbury, to view the lines under General Thomas's command, and will be laden with presents of clothing and trinkets of various kinds when they return to their own people. Mr. John Adams, our member of Congress, was at Major Mifflin's to-day. He came from Roxbury this morning, and to-morrow continues his journey to Philadelphia to join the Continental Congress. The Indians, when told his relations to government, showed signs of curiosity and regarded him with great attention. Mr. Adams is a fine looking man, with a broad, capacious head, seemingly equal to a large amount of brainwork, pleasant though serious expression, a figure a little below the medium in height, and inclining to be stout. He stands among the foremost men in Congress, and his ability to weigh the important matters of state is undoubted. He it is who nominated General Washington for commander-in-chief, and the clearness of his judgment in making that motion is acknowledged by every one.

January 28th. — There is a pamphlet going the rounds which awakens universal interest, and the sentiments are much admired for their boldness and patriotism. The writer is one Thomas Paine, an English Quaker who has been in America a little over a year, but has made acquaintance with Franklin, Samuel Adams, Rush, and other prominent public men. This book was shown to them for criticism, and called by Rush by the title of "Common Sense." It says : —

"The sun never shone on a cause of greater worth. 'T is not the affair of a city, a county, a province, or a kingdom, but of a continent, of at least one eight part of the habitable globe. 'T is not the concern of a day, a year, or an age ; posterity are virtually involved in it even to the end of time. All

SECOND HARVARD, BUILT 1766.

men, whether in England or America, confess that a separation between the countries will take place one time or other. To find out the very time, we need not go far, for the time hath found us. The present, likewise, is that peculiar time which never happens to a nation but once, the time of forming itself into a government. Until we consent that the seat of government in America be legally and authoritatively occupied, where will be our freedom ? Where our property ? Nothing can settle our affairs so expeditiously as an open and determined declaration of independence. The blood of the slain, the weeping voice of nature cries, 't is time to part. A government of our own is our natural right. Freedom hath been hunted round the globe ;

Europe regards her as a stranger; and England hath given her warning to depart. Oh! receive the fugitive and prepare an asylum for mankind."

January 29*th*. — The expedition which left Cambridge last autumn for Canada under command of Benedict Arnold, encountered terrible trials, and many, frightened at the hardships of the march, returned. Those who remained endured almost incredible sufferings; cold, hunger, exhaustion, combined to render them wretched and incapable of service. Their clothes were torn by the forest bushes, their bodies scratched by numberless thorns, and their shoes worn by constant walking over the rough ground, so that many were forced to go barefoot, their food so scarce that many a meal was furnished by the faithful dogs of the party. Here and there a man was left behind to die on the road, as it was impossible to be burdened with helpless invalids. The middle of November the expedition — that part which survived the horrors of the march, reached Quebec, and the third day of last month was joined by General Montgomery, who left the conquered city of Montreal with a subordinate officer, and came to attempt the conquest of the strongest fortified city in America. For several weeks the besieging army surrounded the city, and on the last day of December an assault was made, headed by the brave general. He compelled none to follow him in the attack; he wanted with him "no persons who went with reluctance." To his own soldiers he said: "Men of New York, you will not fear to follow where your general leads. Push on, brave boys; Quebec is ours!" Pressing forward directly in front of the cannon, he was greeted with a volley of grapeshot which laid him dead, and with him his young aid-de-camp, McPherson, and eleven others. Consternation seized the expedition at the fall of its commander, and an immediate retreat was ordered. General Montgomery was an experienced soldier and a valued officer. His loss is mourned all over the country. At news of his death "the whole city of Philadelphia was in tears; every person seemed to have lost his nearest relative or heart friend." Congress publicly expressed for him "their grateful remembrance, profound respect, and high veneration; and desiring to transmit to future ages a truly worthy example of patriotism, conduct, boldness of enterprise, insuperable perseverance, and contempt of danger and death, resolve to rear a marble monument to the glory of Richard Montgomery." Not in public life alone was he beloved and honored; in all the relations of home he was faithful, — kind, upright, modest, every one held him in high esteem. He and his aid-de-camp were buried with military honors by the governor and council of Quebec.

January 30*th*. — Madame Washington has enlivened the monotony of her winter among us by a reception, on the seventeenth anniversary of her wedding day. The fine old Vassall mansion was in gala dress, and the coming and going of guests brightened the sober aspect of the General's head-quarters. The General and his wife stood in the drawing-room at the left of the front entrance, and there received the company. General Washington's study is the room opposite, and opening out of this, the one set apart for his military family. These of course were all thrown open for the accommodation of the guests. There was much chatting and walking to and fro, and easy and social manners were the rule. The General does not talk much, but is gracious and courteous to all. His lady is very unceremonious and easy like other Virginia ladies, though there is no lack of dignity in her manner. Of course simplicity of dress was noticeable, — no jewels or costly ornaments, — though tasteful gowns, daintly trimmed by their owner's fingers, were numerous. The occasion was a most enjoyable one.

February 3d. — How very exact General Washington is, in all the little details of his business! I have a letter, that he wrote to General Sullivan this week, giving directions about the pay of soldiers under his command, which illustrates this : —

"CAMBRIDGE, 28*th Jan.*, 1776.

"D^r S$_{IR}$ I quite forgot to enquire last night (when you were shewing me the Militia Pay Roll) at what rates the officers pay was charged — I am willing to allow them the same pay as the Troops have had and have — that is, to the first of Jany agreeable to the old establishment — (more I cannot) — & For the month of Jany according to the present pay. This is putting of them in all respects up on a footing with the continental army. — You will consider therefore how far this alteration will square with your mode of making up the Pay Rolls, as the manner of charging & extending the sums sh^d appear clear upon the face of the acct^s — I must again desire you to request the Captains to be very correct in making up their acc^{ts} not only because they are to swear to them, but because I must for my own Justification have all the extensions & additions tryed. — Should any of them therefore prove wrong, they will not only give themselves a good deal of trouble & delay for nothing but me also, and I must again desire that they may be cautioned against Including men that have Inlisted into the Continental service, as I will take a good deal of pains to prevent, and if not prevented, to detect an evil, which I am apprehensive will be practiced. If I recollect the Roll you showed me last night men of the same Company and as I suppose from the same Town are charged a different number of days, whereas I think the Ingagement is, that they are to be paid from the time of their marching from the Town — however as I was engaged in reading letters & news papers at the time, I might have mistaken the matter. As I understand the muster Rolls of these Companies (from New Hampshire) are lodged with you I should be glad to receive them with your acct. of the money expended. — If the mileage is drawn for in the manner propos'd by you, the Com^y should be apprised of it, as he told me some of the militia capt^{ns} with out distinguishing of which Government were applying to settle with him.   I am Dr Sir

"Y^r most obed^t serv^t.

"G^e WASHINGTON.

"P. S. If you are not Ingaged I should be glad of your company at dinner at 2 o'clock."

February 4th, Sunday. — Dr. Langdon preached this morning from Micah iv. 5; "For all people will walk every one in the name of his God, and we will walk in the name of the Lord our God forever and ever."

His sermon in the afternoon was from the text: " Lord, when thy hand is lifted up, they will not see : but they shall see, and be ashamed for their envy at the people ; yea, the fire of thine enemies shall devour them." They were warm, earnest discourses, burning with patriotism and loyalty to God. It is a pleasure to listen to the words of our good President, whenever he visits the camp and occupies Dr. Appleton's pulpit.

February 11th. — To-day the pulpit was filled by Rev. Mr. Noble of Newburyport, who preached a good sermon from Revelation xix. 5 : "And a voice came out of the throne, saying, Praise our God all ye his servants, and ye that fear Him, both small and great." The meeting-house was well filled, in spite of the intense cold which crept through the doors and windows, and did its best to turn us all into icicles. The wind whistled its loudest, and blew its heaviest, so that the good minister's voice was often lost in the tumult. Having no cellar under the building, cold feet are the order of the day these wintry Sabbaths, for all who are not provided with a foot-stove, to send its pleasant warmth through the whole body. I wonder when the time will come that the meeting-house will be allowed the comfort of a stove !

February 27th. — General Washington has issued orders, that "all officers, non-commissioned officers, and soldiers, are positively forbid playing at cards and other games of chance. At this time of public distress, men may find enough to do in the service of their God and their country, without abandoning themselves to vice and immorality. As the season is now fast approaching when every man must expect to be drawn into the field of action, it is highly important that he should prepare his mind as well as everything necessary for it. It is a noble cause we are engaged in ; it is the cause of virtue and mankind ; every temporal advantage and comfort to us and our posterity, depends upon the vigor of our exertions ; in short, freedom or slavery must be the result of our conduct ; there can therefore be no greater inducement to men to behave well. But it may not be amiss for the troops to know that if any man in action shall presume to skulk, hide himself, or retreat from the enemy without the orders of his commanding officer, he will be instantly shot down as an example of cowardice ; cowards having too frequently disconcerted the best formed troops by their dastardly behavior." There has been a good deal of card playing and gambling of various kinds. The enforced quiet of the soldiers has been irksome, and they enlivened the monotony in any way they could devise. Many have had opportunity to work at their trades of shoemaking, tailoring, and the like, or to add to their income by selling such things as nuts, apples, and cider, which make a little variety in the daily rations. They are well fed, having a good supply of substantial food — corned beef and pork four days in a week, salt fish one day, and fresh beef two days. As milk is out of the question in the winter, they are allowed one pound and a half of beef, or eighteen ounces of pork every day. A half pint of rice, or a pint of Indian meal, is given them for a week, a quart of spruce beer daily, or nine gallons of molasses to one hundred men per week. Every man has one pound of flour every day except one, in a week, when hard bread takes its place. Butter is given out at the rate of six ounces a week, to each man. Pease, beans, or other vegetables, such as potatoes, turnips, onions, are dealt out in weekly portions. These short winter days, candles are quite a necessary article, and are given every week to the soldiers, six pounds for one hundred men. I have made this schedule of the soldiers' rations, because everything that concerns their comfort has a special interest for me. We seem to be quartered right in the midst of the army, and all the minutiæ of their daily life are an open book before us.

March 2d. — General Washington has been as anxious as any one of the soldiers to attack Boston and dislodge the British troops, but not till now has he felt that he could safely undertake it. Under many difficulties, owing to the hard, frozen ground, works have been thrown up on Lechmere's Point and heavy ordnance placed there. Strong guards are mounted on the works, and everything ready for an attack. I saw some mortars carried over to the Point to-day. The camp begins to look as if battle was resolved upon. Militia from the neighboring towns is pouring in, in response to General Washington's order. Large quantities of fagots and screwed hay are collected for entrenching purposes, and what tells a plainer story than all other preparations, two thousand bandages are in readiness for the wounds which it is expected will need them. About a fortnight ago we had some very severe weather which made strong ice between Dorchester and Boston Neck and also between Roxbury and the Common. General Washington wished to take that opportunity to make the long anticipated assault upon the troops in Boston, by marching our forces over the ice. But the other generals of the council of war thought it hazardous, so the attack has been waiting for a more favorable time.

March 4th, Monday. — Saturday evening the house shook with the roar of cannon which our troops were firing upon poor Boston from Lechmere's Point[1] and Cobble Hill[2] and Roxbury. The British returned the fire, and a shell from their batteries fell on Prospect Hill. Five of our mortars were burst during the bombardment, a great misfortune to us. Yesterday it remained quiet during the day, but the firing began again toward night. Three regiments went from here to Roxbury yesterday and carried some field pieces with them, and cannon also went to Lechmere's Point.

[1] Lechmere's Point, now East Cambridge. — ED.
[2] Cobble Hill, now Somerville. — ED.

March 5th. — Last night about seven o'clock firing began again, and immediately a detachment of two thousand men under command of General Thomas marched to Dorchester Heights and took possession. They moved very quietly and worked so rapidly at the entrenchments, that before daybreak this morning they had raised them high enough to cover themselves from the enemy's shot. These works command Boston, and it is expected that General Howe will think it best to evacuate the town very soon, or else come out to meet our soldiers in battle. To-day is the sixth anniversary of the Boston Massacre, and Washington has inflamed the desire of our men for a contest by saying: "Remember, it is the fifth of March, a day never to be forgotten; avenge the death of your brethren." The hills around Boston are covered with eager and anxious spectators waiting for the conflict. As many as four thousand men are under parade near Fort Number Two, commanded by Old Put, and this afternoon they are to embark in boats near the mouth of the river and attack Boston.

March 6th. — A most furious gale of wind yesterday afternoon prevented the anticipated engagement. To-day the rain pours in torrents, and the wind is very rough. The situation of General Howe and his troops is not enviable. Their fleet cannot ride safely in such a turbulent sea, exposed, besides, to the fire of our batteries on Dorchester Heights. These batteries are a source of wonder to the British, who say "they were raised with an expedition equal to that of the genii belonging to Aladdin's Wonderful Lamp." General Howe thinks "the rebels have done more in one night than his whole army would have done in a month," and believes "it must have been the employment of at least twelve thousand men."

March 7th. — Fast Day. General Washington has issued this order: —

HEAD-QUARTERS, CAMBRIDGE, *March* 6, 1776.

Countersign: Putnam.   *Parole:* Lechmere.

Thursday, the 7th instant, being set apart by the honourable the Legislature of this Province, as a Day of fasting, prayer, and humiliation, "to implore the Lord and Giver of all victory, to pardon our manifold sins and wickednesses and that it would please him to bless the Continental arms with his divine favour and protection," all officers and soldiers are strictly enjoined to pay all due reverence and attention on that day to the sacred duties to the Lord of hosts for his mercies already received and for those blessings which our holiness and uprightness of life can alone encourage us to hope through his mercy to obtain." Our meeting-house was well filled, and Dr. Appleton preached a sermon full of earnestness and devotion, setting before us our manifold causes for humiliation before God.

March 18th. — Boston is free at last. Yesterday General Howe and his entire force sailed away from the wharves in a great number of boats. Immediately General Putnam with several regiments crossed the river and landed at Sewall's Point. Sentinels were apparently standing at their posts on Bunker Hill, but on closer view were found to be wooden men left by the retreating troops to mislead us. When the hoax was discovered a great shout of joy arose, and the cry went out, "Boston is ours! Boston is ours!" The evacuation was looked for several days ago, and was probably hastened by the erection of a battery on Nook's Hill, the part of Dorchester nearest Boston, specially dreaded by General Howe since it completely commands the town. A terrible cannonade was kept up a great part of the time from the first occupation of Dorchester Heights till the departure of the King's troops. To-day General Washington entered the town, accompanied by Mrs. Washington. He has ordered General Heath to assume the command of five regiments and a portion of artillery and march immediately to New York, as it is thought that town will be the next object of British investment. The fleet is still in Nantasket Roads, much to our annoyance.

March 19*th.* — Boston is not much injured, outwardly, I believe. Most of of the houses remain as they were, a few old wooden buildings only having been pulled down for fuel. General Washington will not allow any person to enter the town without a pass, owing to the prevalence of small-pox, and has issued order that "as soon as the selectmen report the town to be cleansed from infection, liberty will be given to those who have business there to go in. The inhabitants belonging to the town will be permitted to return to their habitations, proper persons being appointed at the Neck and at Charlestown Ferry, to grant them passes."

March 20*th.* — The main body of the army entered Boston to-day. As they marched through the streets so long closed against them, doors and windows were crowded with the long imprisoned people, whose faces brightened with welcome as they passed. After eleven months' siege, meaning, as it did for them, cruelty and insult and want, how glad to their ears were the sounds of soldiers' tread, keeping time to the music of Yankee Doodle, and the shouts of American regiments, as cheer after cheer was borne upon the air. With drums beating and colors flying, they traversed the town from end to end. Universal joy prevails at the recovery of this town, which has been contended for by both armies, and which Great Britain considers of enough importance to spend millions of money for its possession.

March 21*st.* — General Washington has issued a proclamation to the people of Boston, and the troops which are quartered there, assuring the former of the good will of the army, and calling upon them to give information of any provisions or military stores that may have been hidden by the retreating army. It also charges the officers to do all in their power to bring peace and good order out of the confusion that reigns at present.

March 23*d.* — The town is open for all who wish to go in, and yesterday an immense concourse of people from all the surrounding country crowded the streets. Many went from curiosity, others to see again the friends and relatives they had so long been parted from. It was very touching to witness the tearful meeting of mothers with their children, of sisters and brothers whom the terrors and sufferings of the past months have kept ignorant of one another's condition. Washington was overwhelmed with expressions of gratitude, and was addressed by the selectmen in the name of the people. They said : " Next to the divine power, we ascribe to your wisdom that this acquisition has been made with so little effusion of human blood." The chief replied in graceful words, commending their wonderful and heroic patriotism and endurance, and ascribing this victory more to the courage and skill of the soldiers than to himself. There have been less than twenty men killed in our army during all the months since Washington assumed the command. This is remarkable : so large a victory at so small a price !

March 27th. — Most of the British fleet, which has been lying outside the harbor for the last ten days, has at last spread its sails and moved away.

HOLLIS HALL, COMPLETED 1763.

This is what Washington has been waiting for, before ordering the army to the south. To-day a brigade under General Sullivan has marched. Congress, on the motion of Mr. John Adams, have " resolved that the thanks of Congress in their own name, and in the name of the Thirteen United Colonies whom they represent, be presented to his Excellency General Washington, and the officers and soldiers under his command, for their wise and spirited conduct in the siege and acquisition of Boston, and that a medal of gold be struck in commemoration of this great event, and presented to his Excellency ; and that a committee of three be appointed to prepare a letter of thanks and a proper device for the medal." Our noble Commander-in-chief has disclaimed all merit of the victory, and transferred the praise to the men under his command. He said : " They were, indeed, at first, a band of undisciplined husbandmen; but it is, under God, to their bravery and attention to duty, that I am indebted for that success which has procured me the only reward I wish to receive — the affection and esteem of my countrymen."

March 29th. — Another address of congratulation and commendation to General Washington. This from the two branches of the legislature combined. They say: "Go on, still go on, approved by Heaven, — revered by all good men, and dreaded by tyrants; may future generations, in the peaceful enjoyment of that freedom which your sword shall have established, raise the most lasting monuments to the name of Washington." Yesterday he attended the long-established Thursday lecture, which Boston has kept up since the days of Winthrop and Wilson, but which the troubles of the last months have interrupted. It was a season of joyful gratitude to God, who had delivered this New England Zion from the power of its oppressor, and had brought peace and quietness once more into its homes. The good old town they call "a tabernacle that should never be taken down, of which not one of the stakes should ever be removed, nor one of the cords be broken."

April 4th. — To-day General Washington has left Cambridge and gone to New York. All the troops, with the exception of five regiments under the command of General Ward, have left with him. It is feared that the British fleet may return, after putting us off our guard, and works are building rapidly in defense of the harbor. General Ward has stationed two regiments in Boston, one at Dorchester Heights, one at Charlestown, and one at Beverly.

April 7th, Sunday. — Dr. Appleton preached to-day from Proverbs xxii. 1: "A good name is rather to be chosen than great riches, and loving favor rather than silver and gold." A beautiful sermon, alluding tenderly and with reverence to our beloved Commander-in-chief, who has gloriously earned all the affection which is lavished upon him, whose name will live in New England hearts forever, as that of our deliverer from slavery. The good Doctor applied the text to us individually and as a nation, urging us to see to it that history, as she sends our record to the future, writes only of truth, godliness, and courage, untainted by covetousness, or cowardice, or deceit.

Boston, April 10th. — Here I am in our much-suffering town, which is cleared at last of its persecutors. Mrs. McHenry invited me to accompany her husband and herself yesterday to spend a few days with her sister, and I gladly embraced the opportunity. The eight miles' ride seemed longer than ever in our impatience to stand once more in the streets consecrated by the blood of martyrs. At the Neck we passed the British fortifications, and looked upon the works on Dorchester Heights, which were so great a source of terror to General Howe's troops, and which effectually drove them away from our shores. We rode through Orange and Newbury streets [1] to

---

[1] Orange, Newbury, Marlborough streets and Cornhill formed what is now Washington Street. — ED.

Hanover Square,[1] and there our eyes were saddened by the sight of — not the grand old Liberty Tree which has spread its limbs for more than a hundred years — but only its stump. Of all the magnificent trees in this elm neighborhood, this was the finest of them all, but its name and the remembrance of the many treasonable acts it has sanctioned in Liberty Hall,[2] were enough to enlist against it the detestation of British soldiers. Last August it fell a victim to the ax, and provided for the comfort of its destroyers full fourteen cords of wood. From Newbury Street we passed into Marlborough Street, and stopped in front of the Old South Church. This has been desecrated by the soldiers, who used it as a riding school, covering the floors with many hundred cart-loads of gravel, after removing the pulpit and pews, which they used as fuel. Many of the valuable papers and books of Rev. Thomas Prince, which were kept in the tower, were used to kindle fires for the lawless soldiery, and the parsonage adjoining, with several noble sycamore trees in front, were pulled down for firewood.

Turning toward our left hand, the Old Province House reared its stately walls before us, every brick of which was made thousands of miles away in Holland, and was brought across the rolling ocean nearly a hundred years ago, by Mr. Peter Sargeant, whose initials, with the year of its erection, stand forth prominently in the iron fence which surmounts the portico : —

16 P. S. 79

How many governors, appointed by his Majesty to rule our new rebellious Colony, have, during the last sixty years, ascended those massive steps! Often have they stood upon the balcony in front to address the throng of loyal colonists in the street below, and in response to their loud huzzas, bowed in courtly dignity. The old building remains the same as when they held their grand levees within its fine apartments, and received homage as viceroys of the King, but we fondly believe that the times have so far changed that Sir William Howe will be the very last of his Majesty's representatives whose authority will be respected in Massachusetts. Here he held consultation with General Gage before the disastrous battle of Bunker Hill, and from the cupola which crowns the summit, he watched the approach of our besieging army, before which, at last, he beat an ignominious retreat. The gilded Indian which acts as weather-vane, was pointing his arrow directly east as we passed, and over him and the mansion he faithfully guarded, floated our Union flag of thirteen stripes. Continuing our journey through Marlborough Street to the State House, above which waved the same glorious banner, we looked down King Street, where the memorable Massacre took place six years ago. Up Cornhill, past the shop of Paul Revere, the intrepid patriot and skilful mechanic, into Queen Street, and then we paused at the foot of Pemberton Hill. The hill is terraced, and

---

[1] Hanover Square, where Essex, Washington, and Boylston streets meet. — ED.
[2] The ground around the tree was familiarly known as Liberty Hall. — ED.

a long flight of steps leads to the magnificent mansion on its brow.[1] The grounds are tastefully laid out, nature and art uniting to make this one of the finest private residences in Boston. Lord Percy, I believe, lived here during a part of his stay in town. Then we passed on to our destination on Beacon Hill. Mrs. McHenry's sister, Mrs. Elwyn, received us most cordially. Her home is not far from Mr. Hancock's house, and overlooks the Common, which affords pasturage for numberless cows, which make continual music with the tinkling of their bells and their contented lowing from morning till night. These fifty acres of hills and valleys reach from the granary graveyard on the one side, to the ebb and flow of the busy Charles river, which washes the lower end. Grand old trees shade its walks in the summer months, and now are beginning to awake after a winter's sleep, and put forth delicate buds in token of life. The great elm which has watched the growth of the town from its earliest settlement, is still as strong and full of vigor as ever. This morning we have been sauntering through the grounds so lately covered with the camp of the British troops. Walked up Frog Lane to Common Street, and turned into Blott's Lane, past the house of Sam Adams; thence back to the enclosure, crossing which we found ourselves in front of Mr. Hancock's house, which was occupied by General Clinton and Lord Percy at different times during the siege. The house and stables were both used for the wounded after Bunker Hill battle. The magnificent mansion, standing, as it does, on the brow of the hill, commanding an extensive view of the country around, is typical of the prominence and exalted station of its owner, who has incurred the deadly displeasure of the royal government, by reason of his determined patriotism. After the Lexington affair the house was pillaged by the soldiers, who broke down the fences and did some slight damage in other ways. It has been repaired, however, and looks now as in the good old days before British tyranny crushed our liberties to the ground. The same massive stone walls, supporting a tiled roof, from which several dormer windows look forth upon the town and its surroundings; the same projecting balcony over the front door; the same broad stone steps and paved walk leading from the street, so often trodden by old Thomas Hancock and pranced over by the boyish feet of President Hancock, thirty years ago. We went over the house, into the grand drawing-room at the right, where hang portraits of the Hancock family, back to the days of the early Puritans; into the immense dining-hall opening out of this, designed for large companies; into the family drawing-room at the left of the entrance, and the smaller dining-room out of it, and through the spacious halls and chambers elegantly furnished and hung with pictures of various kinds. Things are not injured nearly as much as was feared. The furniture and pictures are in good condition. This afternoon Mrs. Elwyn took us to drive through the North End. We passed

[1] Afterwards the residence of Gardner Greene. — ED.

through Common Street[1] to School Street, and stopped at King's Chapel. Here we found ourselves on the oldest ground probably, built upon in Boston. The British officers worshipped in the chapel during the occupation of Boston by their troops, and when they evacuated the town, Dr. Caner, its rector, went with them to Halifax, taking with him all the church registers, plate, and vestments. His residence is just north of the chapel. We alighted at the old burying ground, and walked reverently among the graves, some of them a century old; read the inscription upon the monument to Rev. John Cotton, the first minister of the church, as well as that of old Governor Winthrop of beloved memory. On Long Acre we rode over the same ground where, one year ago this month, Lord Percy's brigade formed in line of march to hasten to the assistance of the royal troops in Lexington. Looking down School Street the old Latin School rose before us. Here Dr. Franklin went to school for a year, and John Hancock was taught in childhood. The appearance of Percy's troops on that memorable April morning, stretching their glittering length past School Street, was the signal to dismiss the awe-struck scholars who, as a school, have never met since. We rode through Tremont Street into Gay Alley,[2] and paused a moment at the handsome new church, built only four years ago. Dr. Cooper, its pastor, a true-hearted patriot, left Boston after Lexington fight, and General Gage quartered a British regiment here for a while. But services were sometimes held in Brattle Church during the siege. It did not escape in the bombardment of the town, having been struck by a twenty-four pound cannon ball from our batteries at Lechmere's Point. At our right stood Faneuil Hall, the Cradle of Liberty, whose walls have echoed the burning words of Otis, and Adams, and Warren. Turning into Middle Street,[3] we passed the residence of Dr. Warren, where, as a skilful physician, no less than a warm and earnest patriot, he attracted to himself the affection and esteem of his townsmen. In our ride we passed the Orange Tree Tavern,[4] the houses of Paul Revere and James Otis, and the Green Dragon Tavern, where "treasonable" meetings were held by Boston mechanics for the purpose of conferring as to the best methods of thwarting the movements of the Tories and the British soldiers. These meetings were very secret, the subject discussed being made known to only a few of the leading patriots, like Hancock, Adams, Warren, Otis, Church. But unaccountable as it seemed, General Gage was always informed of their movements, and not till the arrest of Dr. Church did the mystery explain itself. Then it was easy to trace the treachery.

The North Church was full of interest to us as the place where the lanterns hung and flashed forth their warning light to the eyes of the waiting

---

[1] Common Street, Long Acre, and Tremont Street, are now Tremont Street. — ED.
[2] Gay Alley, an old name for Brattle Street. — ED.
[3] Now Hanover Street. — ED.
[4] The Orange Tree Tavern stood on what is now the corner of Court and Hanover Streets. — ED.

Paul Revere, on the evening of April 18, 1775.[1] On the opposite Charlestown shore he paced impatiently back and forth, casting many a look toward the spire which for fifty years had pointed upward with steady finger. At last the signal flamed forth through the darkness, and the midnight rider sprang to his horse and was off on his patriotic errand. Here on Copp's Hill were British redoubts, behind which, June 17th, our soldiers on Bunker Hill were fired upon, and on that day so full of disaster to the royal troops, the hill and all houses near were covered with eager spectators of the battle. General Gage witnessed the affair from the steeple of the North Church, they say. I must not forget the graves in Copp's Hill Cemetery, through which we walked. Here are buried Dr. Increase Mather and his son Rev. Cotton Mather, and many others, who have filled places of honor in church and state. Some of the graves are fully a hundred and fifty years old. Major Pitcairn of Lexington fame, who was killed at Bunker Hill by the bullet of a negro soldier, is interred under Christ Church. They say the British major was a brave officer, just and impartial in his treatment of his soldiers, and greatly beloved by them. He fell mortally wounded into the arms of his son, who bore him in a boat across the river, to a house near the ferry. General Gage, it is said, sent his own physician to attend him, but he lived but a short time. We passed the fine old mansion of Governor Hutchinson, which was so injured by the mob ten years ago, during the Stamp Act troubles. Thomas Hutchinson was held in high esteem before the tyrannical conduct of the mother country aroused the spirit of liberty in our Colonies, and the part he played at the beginning of the contest, made him as offensive as before he had been popular. He departed for England two years ago, leaving this grand old house built by his father, the place of his birth and residence for nearly sixty-five years. It is built of brick, with six Corinthian pilasters in front and the crown of Great Britain surmounting each window. The interior is replete with magnificence, and the grounds are extensive and tasteful. The Governor's library, which was of great value, including many choice manuscripts,

---

[1] "Impatient to mount and ride,
Booted and spurred, with a heavy stride
On the opposite shore walked Paul Revere.
Now he patted his horse's side,
Now gazed at the landscape far and near,
Then, impetuous, stamped the earth,
And turned and tightened his saddle-girth;
But mostly he watched with eager search
The belfry-tower of the old North Church,
As it rose above the graves on the hill,
Lonely and spectral and sombre and still.
And lo! as he looks, in the belfry's height
A glimmer, and then a gleam of light!
He springs to the saddle, the bridle he turns,
But lingers and gazes, till full on his sight
A second lamp in the belfry burns." — *Longfellow*.

and the furniture which was rich and costly, were destroyed by the enraged mob, August 26, 1765.

[LETTER FROM DOROTHY DUDLEY TO MISS ESTHER LIVINGSTONE.]

CAMBRIDGE, *April 19th,* 1776.

MY DEAREST ESTHER, — Your long-promised visit to our little town not made yet! I am impatient to show you its beauties now that spring is peeping at us with tearful eyes while all the time her face is rippling with laughter. You know that this is the first anniversary of the never-to-be-forgotten day which began the dreadful war that is upon us. This year has been one of severe trial for us all. Of course there has been reason for great economy both in household expenses and in dress. Tea is a comfort put from us with resolution, though its absence from our tables is cuttingly felt by many. As far as it is possible we patronize only home manufactures, and ourselves use the spindle to diminish the necessity for foreign material. The residence among us of so large a body of soldiers has made our life in some sense a military one, our hands, our sympathies, and our time having been devoted to their interests. I find, in looking over my diary, that the entries are almost without exception relating to the doings of the army,[1] and, indeed were you with us you would not wonder at this. There have been no interests separate from the soldiers', or I ought to say from our country's. Your letter received by Major Heath was very welcome. I am glad you have so warm a friendship with Mrs. Hancock. Her sister, Miss Katy Quincy, is expecting to go to Philadelphia in a few weeks, and I hope you will make her acquaintance. She is somewhat older than Mrs. Hancock, who is, I think, the youngest of the family. Mrs. Judge Sewall, you know, is another sister. They are a charming family, and Mr. Quincy is a devoted father, warmly beloved by them all.

You ask for descriptions of some of the persons of note that have favored our town with their presence. First and foremost of all I place our Commander-in-chief, but I am sure you already know from other sources his characteristics, mental and physical. I will only say he has a fine face, a noble manner, and is the personification of truth and uprightness. General Charles Lee you have seen, and need no words of mine to bring before you his tall, lank figure and prominent features, marked by uniform carelessness of the opinion of others. "Old Put" is a rough, fiery genius, ready for hard work whenever and wherever it presents itself, spurring his men on to great achievements, and beloved by them all, because of the good, honest heart hidden behind the prickly burr. General Nathaniel Greene, who has had command under General Lee at Prospect Hill, is the only general, they say, that showed his pleasure at the appointment of Washington to the chief command by addressing words of welcome to him for himself and soldiers upon his arrival at Cambridge. He was a Quaker before the war

[1] The Editor has already expressed his suspicion that another reason may be suggested for this.

called out his fighting genius and awoke his slumbering patriotism. He took his first lessons in the military school by watching the British soldiers exercise on Boston Common, and followed them up by vigorous study of books and military life as he saw it around him. He learned so rapidly that few generals stand higher in the confidence of his peers than General Greene. He is rather a large man, with a face indicating fire and firmness, tempered by the innate goodness which looks out of his clear, quiet eyes. General Harry Knox is his most intimate and trusted friend. The two were almost constantly together in days when both were studying the art of war, and Mr. Knox kept a bookstore on Cornhill. He, like his friend, is the soul of honor, gentle as well as brave, and possessed of a manly heart brimming with benevolence. You know our veterans, Ward and Pomeroy, and are well acquainted with that queer little man, our excellent quartermaster-general, Thomas Mifflin, who is the right man in the right place, every one agrees. General John Stark, who so distinguished himself in the French war, has won commendation by the part he has played this year. At the alarm of war he hastily formed a regiment in New Hampshire and marched immediately for our camp; figured bravely at Bunker Hill, and, with his impetuous nature boiling for action, he has been on tiptoe for battle ever since. He looks much like an Indian with his high cheek-bones and prominent nose, and tall, erect figure, and his soul is as full of courage and as impatient of restraint as that of any wild son of the forest. His wife, Molly Stark, as he familiarly calls her, followed her husband to camp, and when our troops occupied Dorchester Heights, at his desire she mounted a horse to watch the passage of his regiment over the river to West Boston, and to be ready at a moment's notice to spread the alarm, if opposition arose. Are they not a well-mated pair? General Sullivan is a popular officer, a good soldier, and a pleasant gentleman. His quarters were at Winter Hill. I might go on and enumerate officers who hold honorable places in the services, Preble, Heath, Patterson, Arnold, Gates, and others, not as well known; but I fear you will tire of the list.

I thank you for your pleasant pictures of Philadelphia life and sketches of the prominent figures there. Some of your great men belong to us. The venerable Franklin, the two Adamses, and your excellent President of Congress, we claim by right of birth. The patriot Sam Adams, the "stirrer up of the Revolution," with his nervous energy of tongue and pen, his wit and sarcasm, his dignity and integrity and magnanimity, is second to no one in the weight of his influence. His tall, graceful figure and courteous bearing are very familiar to Boston people, as are also the features and character of John Hancock.

Our winter has been a very quiet one, but little disturbed by the roar of cannon and the terrors of bloodshed. But few dinner parties or receptions have broken the monotony. I have been twice to Major Mifflin's; once in December to meet Mrs. John Adams; again in January, when her husband was present. Mrs. Adams I cannot enough admire. There is evidence of a mind of uncommon clearness, sharpened by reading and study, and a heart warm and true, while her graceful accomplishments make her a lady of more than common attractions. Her husband you know. They seem to be admirably suited to one another. Mrs. Washington held a levee in January and I was honored with an invitation. Colonel Vassall's house is perhaps the most elegant and spacious in New England,[1] and the reception was everything one could wish. No display, no extravagance ; but simple taste suited to the time of universal economy, characterized all the arrangements. The magnificent rooms, elaborately carved and panelled, are becomingly furnished, though I believe the whole house is not in common use.

Mrs. Morgan, wife of Dr. Morgan, who is in traitor Church's place as director-general of the hospital, Mrs. Mifflin, Mrs. Remington, Mrs. Custis, Mrs. Gates, Mrs. Trowbridge, Mrs. Appleton and her daughters, Mrs. McHenry, Mrs. Wigglesworth, Mrs. Hastings and Miss Rebecca Hastings, and many others whom you do not know, were there. Several officers were also present. It was much like the companies at Major Mifflin's, in numbers, and many of the faces were the same.

The event of the spring, the joy which has crowned the patient waiting of the winter, is the evacuation of Boston by General Sir William Howe and his Majesty's troops. It was accomplished with so little bloodshed that we have deep cause for gratitude. Among the throng who greeted Washington on his triumphant entry to the town, March 18th, there were none in sorrow for the loss of dear friends. There have been less than two hundred American lives lost in battle during all the months that British and New England armies have been confronting one another, and now our Colony, we hope and believe, is freed from the incubus that has weighed upon her so long, and it only remains to push from the harbor all remnants of the British navy, to be once more at liberty to breathe. You cannot know what a relief it is to be able to go and come, feeling sure that the Redcoats are at a distance, and not likely to burden us again with their presence. Boston is not injured nearly as much as was feared, owing to the orders of General Howe, who allowed no plundering unless the necessities of the army called for it, and whose orders were so strict as to punish with death any disobedience of this command. The soldiers were obliged to pay due attention to dress, and to never appear at parade "without having the hair properly and smoothly clubbed." The officers must wear sashes on duty, and none were to appear under arms with tobacco in their mouths. This one of General Howe's orders gives us a little glimpse of life in the British camp. "The commanding officer is surprised to find the necessity of repeating orders, that long since ought to have been complied with, as the men on all duties appear in the following manner. viz: hair not smooth and badly powdered, several without slings to their firelocks, hats not bound, pouches in a shame-

---

[1] It is evident that Miss Dudley had not seen the Pepperell and Sparhawk houses at Kittery. — ED.

ful and dirty condition, no frills to their shirts, and their linen very dirty, leggings hanging in a slovenly manner about their knees, some men without uniform stocks, and their arms and accoutrements by no means so clean as they ought to be. These unsoldierlike neglects must be immediately remedied."

I have been spending a few days in Boston with Mrs Elwyn, and drove about the town to look at the changes which have gone on under the British rule. The North End is very interesting to me as the place where many plans for the furtherance of American liberty were hatched. Paul Revere and Joseph Warren and James Otis lived in that quarter. At Copp's Hill we drove up to the cemetery just as a funeral procession was winding its way into the enclosure. It was that of a man in the prime of life, as we learned afterwards, a Mr. John Williston, who died from the effects of privations during the siege. Dr. Mather Byles, who has been pastor of Hollis Street Church for more than forty years, made a prayer at the grave, and Robert Newman, the sexton of Christ Church, was in attendance. Remembering your passion for epitaphs, I copied several from the grave-stones, some of them black with age. Here is one : —

"Time, what an empty vapor 'tis,
And days, how swift they fley!
Our life is ever on the wing,
And death is ever nigh.
The moment when our lives begin,
We all begin to die."

Here is another from a stone more than half a century old : " Life's little stage is a small eminence, inch high, the grave above — that home of man where dwells the multitude. We gaze around, we read their monuments, we sigh ; and while we sigh, we sink, and are what we deplore." These lines were on an old monument without name or date, and it was with difficulty I could decipher the words : —

"What is't fond mortal yt thou would'st obtain
By spinning out a painful life of cares;
Thou livest to act thy childhood o're again,
And naught intends but grief and seeing years.
Who leaves this world like me, just in my prime,
Speeds all my business in a * * * time."

I paused at a little grave, my eye caught by my own name, Dorothy, and read on the sunken, aged stone, that

DORYTHY GREENOUGH
AGED 4 YEARS & 8 MONTHS
DYED YE 20 OCTOBER 1667.

You have heard of Dr. Byles, who is so distinguished for his wit and wisdom. He is a descendant of Richard Mather and John Cotton. His son, Mather Byles, Jr., rector of Christ Church, was so determined a royalist that

Dr. Byles and his Preaching. 71

he left his flock and sailed for Halifax with the King's troops. The old Doctor was very non-committal in politics, rarely mentioning them, and never introducing the subject in the pulpit. When asked why he so steadfastly avoided it, he said : " I have thrown up four breastworks, behind which I have entrenched myself, neither of which can be enforced. In the first place, I do not understand politics ; in the second place, you all do, every man and mother's son of you ; in the third place, you have politics all the week, pray let one day in seven be devoted to religion ; in the fourth place, I am engaged in work of infinitely greater importance ; give me any subject to preach on of more consequence than the truth I bring to you, and I will preach on it, the next Sabbath."

His preaching is very effective, savoring of earnestness and sincerity, and filled with the truth of the Gospel. His manner, too, is attractive, and his voice powerful and melodious. Out of the pulpit he is brimming over with fun, never at a loss for a repartee, and quick to see the ludicrous. It is said that in his young days he made advances to a lady who refused to favor his suit. Afterwards she married a Mr. Quincy, and Dr. Byles, the next time he saw her, remarked : " So, madam, it appears that you prefer a Quincy to Byles." " Yes," she replied, " for if there had been anything worse than biles, God would have afflicted Job with them." At one time, the road in front of his house was in a very bad condition, so that in wet weather the mud was much like the slough we read about in Bunyan's " Pilgrim's Progress." All his efforts to arouse the town government to remedy the trouble were without success. One day, two of the selectmen, the very ones who had charge of the streets, in riding past the house, found themselves stuck in the mud, and were obliged to alight from the carriage to extricate it from the slough. As they did so, the tall, commanding figure of Dr. Byles appeared before them, and bowing gracefully and respectfully, he said : " Gentlemen, I have often complained to you of this nuisance, without any attention being paid to it, and I am very glad to see you *stirring* in this matter now." The good old Doctor has made many an enemy by his unsparing sarcasm, which he cannot forbear using, even if it cuts its victim to the quick. His family are determined loyalists, every one ; and public opinion says, if Dr. Mather Byles did not close his mouth so tight, in political matters, Tory principles would be sure to find utterance.

Dr. Byles is a poet of no mean fame, having written many verses of both a serious and trifling nature. On one occasion Governor Belcher, who was a warm friend and admirer of the Doctor's, invited him to visit the Province of Maine in his company. Doctor Byles declined, but the Governor, nothing daunted by the refusal, set himself to work to devise some way of securing the wished-for pleasure. He persuaded the punning parson[1] to take

---

[1] Dr.Byles's humor is celebrated in a poetical account of the clergy of Boston, quoted by Mr. Samuel Kettell, in his *Specimens of American Poetry* : —

" There's punning Byles, provokes our smiles,
A man of stately parts;

tea, one Sabbath afternoon, on board the *Scarborough* ship-of-war, and as the friends were cosily seated at table, engaged in conversation and quaffing fragrant draughts of steaming hyson, slowly but surely the ship was carrying them out to sea. When the Doctor discovered the stratagem, he resigned himself to the voyage with a very good grace. The next Sabbath, in lack of a suitable hymn for service at sea, he composed a very excellent one, the first stanza of which I remember: —

> "Great God, thy works our wonder raise;
> To thee our swelling notes belong;
> While skies, and winds, and rocks, and seas,
> Around shall echo to our song."

Almost every Tory has taken his departure from Boston with the British soldiers. There are none to be seen in the streets in this time of general thanksgiving, and except for the manifest signs of suffering consequent upon the reign of war, the town looks as in the far away days of peace.

April 20th. — If you were with me this lovely spring day we would persuade Tony Vassall, the quondam coachman of Mrs. Penelope Vassall, to drive us about the town. It seems very lonely since the tents have disappeared, and with them the soldiers whose busy life was incorporated with our own for nearly a twelve-month. Since you cannot see Cambridge as it looks to-day, let my eyes do service instead, and, if you enlist your imagination, perhaps you will be able to discern the picture, First, you must look at our college halls, now vacant. They rear their walls of brick as proudly as if conscious of their importance to the world of letters. You know they did good service during the last year, sheltering nearly two thousand soldiers from the snows and blows of winter. We will let Tony drive us slowly past the meeting-house, where Dr. Nathaniel Appleton has preached for twenty years, and for nearly forty years previous in the old meeting-house, of which this takes the place. Dr. Increase Mather preached his installation sermon, and Dr. Cotton Mather extended the right hand of fellowship. The good Doctor has lived for more than fourscore years, and we fear he must leave us before long. Here the first Provincial Congress of Massachusetts was held, until adjourned to Watertown, and here for many years the College Commencements were celebrated in midsummer. Look across the road to the court-house, which lifts its tower high in the air as a warning, perhaps, to miscreants. We turn the corner, past the stately tree which for years has outstretched its sheltering arms over the heads of passing man and beasts, and come abruptly upon

> He visits folks to crack his jokes,
> Which never mend their hearts.
>
> "With strutting gait, and wig so great,
> He walks along the streets,
> And throws out wit, or what's like it,
> To every one he meets." — E.D.

The Wigglesworth House.

the president's house, which has harbored all the revered men who stood at the head of the College Faculty since President Wadsworth. Riding slowly toward the south we come next to Professor Wigglesworth's house, which is very old, having been built, I have heard, by old President Leverett, before this century came in. The worthy professor is a great student, as was his father, the first Hollis Professor of Divinity in the college, and, in proof of this, there is a hole worn through the floor by their feet under the desk of the room used, by father and son, as a study. Next to this interesting house is the old parsonage, which has stood for a hundred years ; the residence of Dr. Urian Oakes, who was not only pastor of the church, but college president as well ; of Rev. Nathaniel Gookin and Rev. William Brattle, as well as our present beloved and aged pastor, Dr. Appleton. This venerable house has undergone some repairs which have materially altered its appearance and freshened its life. Long may it stand as a reminder of the lives of the holy men who have done so much for Cambridge by their influence and their labors.

Now Tony will turn the horse's head toward the right and we will ride down to Butler's Hill, past Mr. Dana's house, which is a noble mansion set in the midst of orchards and grounds which are finely cultivated. Further down we come to Mr. Inman's estate, which, since the departure of the soldiers, has been occupied by two ladies, one of them Miss Betsey Murray, a niece of Mrs. Inman's, though the fact of her being there is a secret, known only to a few. Mr. Ralph Inman you have often heard of as one of the aristocrats of our town, and members of Christ Church. Mrs. Inman is really a remarkable woman. She belongs to the Murray family, which proudly dates back to the Norman conquest in England, and claims kindred blood with the Philiphaugh family of Murrays in Selkirkshire. She is a stanch Scotch woman, and has the energy of character and charming frankness and honesty so common to that people. She has crossed the ocean many times in company with her brother, Mr. James Murray, a gentleman of upright character and great success as a merchant. She has been three times married ; to Mr. Inman about five years since. When she was Elizabeth Murray, I have been told that she carried on business in a shop, corner of Queen Street and Cornhill in Boston, and made for herself a very comfortable income, and during her first two marriages she continued the business, and still owns the building. Her property, acquired by her own exertions, is considerable, and her husband, Mr. Smith, left her his whole estate, so that she has had all the comforts and luxuries of wealth. She is classed among the Tories because of her associations with the British officers of government, her husband, Mr. Inman, having been an addresser to General Gage last year. Her education and social advantages have united to make her a most delightful companion, and one whose presence was eagerly sought. She has remained in this vicinity during all the troubles, though Mr. Inman fled into Boston, and owing to her acquaintance with **General Putnam**, Major Mifflin, and others among our officers, has been secured from molestation by our soldiers. I heard to-day that General Putnam deputed his son to remain in Cambridge on the day of Bunker Hill battle, to guard Mrs. Inman — a proof certainly of the high regard he entertained for her.

The house is large and elegant in its appointments, but now the air of carelessness which is visible around the place is very sad. Barracks disfigure the eastern border of the grounds, and here and there we come upon traces of soldiers' life. Everywhere in our ride we see the evidences of war. Cambridge lines stretch themselves from Butler's Hill to the river, and forts are plentifully sprinkled over the town for our protection. Turning our house around (for at Mr. Inman's farm we find ourselves at the limit of civilization in Cambridge), we drive back to Butler's Hill. On this eminence you can have a good view of our fortified town. Do you see that redoubt at our left, just at the bend of the river? That is Fort Number One.[1] We would drive around by it and follow the course of the river to the causeway from Boston, if the road was sufficiently travelled to render it pleasant riding. But only heavy country wagons laden with produce ever come into this part of our village. So Tony gives the pony a smart touch with the whip, and soon we are in front of Colonel Phipps's handsome house whose grounds extend down to the river. Colonel David Phipps is a brother, you know, of Mrs. Vassall, Mrs. Lee, Mrs. Lechmere, and Mrs. Boardman. His house was taken last spring when he left the town for Boston, and was used as a hospital during the summer. Look at those wooden Indians standing guard upon the gate posts, barbarous in dress and expression, deliberately taking aim with unerring arrow at the heads of unwelcome guests. They are a source of terror to many childish minds, believing, as they do, that these savage sentinels are specially devoted to the destruction of naughty children; and the road past their domain is traversed by flying feet when necessity makes it a road to duty.

Pursuing our journey, we pass the house some people say President Dunster occupied at one time, though he lived, I believe, in the old college house in the college yard during most of his presidency; through the square to Judge Remington's house, past the jail and the jailer's house to the road which is the thoroughfare from Boston. Looking down toward the river you see the tavern kept by Ebenezer Bradish, so popular an inn particularly at Commencement seasons, and which the students were wont to patronize so freely. Here we are at the borders of the Brattle grounds, which are unique in their elegance, and which by the departure of both father and son are left to be used by our government. They extend down to the river, and toward the west to the estate of the Widow Vassall. A private driveway leads up to the substantial house which stands as sentinel in the centre of the grounds. We will turn to the right and pass again the court-

---

[1] Present site of The Riverside Press. — ED.

house, and meeting-house, old Massachusetts, Stoughton, and Harvard, little Holden Chapel, and Hollis halls, till we reach the gambrel-roofed house,[1] which shields itself behind a row of Lombardy poplars, at the further limits of the college green, beyond the road to Charlestown. This is Mr. Hastings's house, famous as the head-quarters of the Committee of Safety, and honored often by the presence of Washington during his residence in Cambridge. On the opposite side of the Common we see the magnificent widespreading elm immortalized by our Commander-in-chief, when, standing beneath its shade the third day of last July, he formally assumed the command of all the troops of the Colonies. In a line with this giant tree stand two others which for a century and more have been silent witnesses of the life of the village. These three venerable elms saw the uprising of the old wooden

HOLDEN CHAPEL.

building where gathered the nucleus of Harvard College; they heard the ringing of the desecrating axe as it laid low many of their companions of the forest, and looked on, as the seminary, growing in proportions as in years, added, one by one, the more imposing structures which now stand within the college yard. How many stories they could tell us, were their long silence to be broken, of the men of the past who have walked beneath their shade, and how many secrets would be unlocked to us which will never be recorded on history's page! Beneath one of them, the next neighbor to the Washington elm, stood Rev. George Whitefield,[2] I am told, when, thirty years

---

[1] The Holmes house. — ED.

[2] This tree, afterwards known as the Whitefield elm, was destroyed a few years ago by the city authorities because it was considered an interruption to the travel on Garden Street. A respite of a few years had been granted it at the earnest solicitation of some to whom the monarchs of the "forest

ago, he visited Cambridge and preached to the students of Harvard. How the venerable tree must have echoed with the eloquence of the gifted preacher, as with burning words he pleaded with his hearers who thronged the Common, beseeching them for Christ's sake to be reconciled to God. North of the Hastings house lived Mr. Moses Richardson, one of the three brave men who were killed one year ago to-day and were so hastily buried in the rude grave within the old cemetery. Dr. Warren little thought, when with sympathizing words he promised a better burial to them, to soothe the grief-stricken friends, that he himself would so soon lie low, away from the terrors and trials of earth. Some time we hope to raise a stone to commemorate their patriotism and heroic death. Further up the road to Menotomy lives Captain Walton of the militia, whose company was out, of course, on that day of terror. Tony himself has a snug little home on this road, where with his wife, Lucy, and Darby his wide-awake seven-year-old, he has lived since the flight of his mistress. But few houses are scattered along this road. Mr. Frost's house, a good way beyond, sheltered a number of soldiers while the army was stationed in Cambridge. He, I believe, built the house which Rev. Mr. Serjeant, rector of Christ Church, occupied for a time, and which we are passing now in going from Menotomy Road to Christ Church. Let us ride further, for I would like you to see Church Row, or Tory Row, as latterly it has been called. The Brattle estate we touch, on its western border, as we ride past, Widow Vassall's on our left and Colonel John Vassall's on our right. I mention these houses by the names of their Tory owners, but in reality they have passed from their hands and are now used by our government. General Washington has a glorious view from his windows in the magnificent house of his choice. The blue hills stretch their hazy length for several miles along the opposite shore of the river. To-day the sun lights up the dimpling stream with numberless diamond flashes, and over the whole landscape he has thrown a bright halo of glory. Next above our General's head-

primeval" are dear, and the feeling of regret and almost of indignation at its final sacrifice was extensive. This sentiment found expression in some lines attributed to the Rev. Nicholas Hoppin, D. D., for many years rector of Christ Church, two of which are appended. — ED.

"Thy room was wanted, huge old Elm,
  Magnate of Nature's realm!
Thou hast stood forth too long,
  Putting thy pillared strength
Our rattling courts among;
  And thou hast met thy doom at length,
Deserving a lament in nobler song!

"Down, then, with thy enormous bulk,
  Thy crazed unwieldly hulk!
This time of rushing haste
  Will not abide the old;
Has not a thought to waste
  On bygone memories idly told,
Nor brooks one obstacle from age misplaced."

quarters we come to the sometime residence of Judge Richard Lechmere,[1] and later of Judge Jonathan Sewall, both aristocrats and Tories, who left town some time ago. The Phipps farm, which comprises the eastern part of Cambridge, passed into the hands of Judge Lechmere on his marriage with Miss Phipps, and it is known often as Lechmere's Point, celebrated as the place of landing of the Redcoats under Pitcairn and Smith, as intent on an errand of destruction they left Boston one year ago last night. Judge Sewall is a genial, upright gentleman — an intimate friend of our own John Adams, though Jonathan and John have politically walked far apart of late. Judge Sewall is now in England. The house is one of the best on this highway, which has none but elegant mansions to grace its borders. The limits of the

THE SEWALL-RIEDESEL MANSION, BEFORE ITS ALTERATION.

Sewall estate bring us to Judge Joseph Lee's, where the courteous and affable gentleman still lives. Though forced to resign his position as councillor in the troubles of September, 1774, he was allowed to remain in his home, provided he would not interfere in politics. This he readily promised, and thus retains the noble house which he has owned for nearly twenty years. It is very old, but substantial in its building, looking as if it would outlive many of the younger houses which are hastily erected in this generation. He bought it, I have heard, of the widow of Cornelius Waldo and on a window pane is found, scratched with a diamond, the name of Daniel Waldo (Rev.). The frame of this mansion was brought from England, not because Massachusetts had no trees, but because it was feared that capable workmen could not be found to put it together to suit the fastidious taste of its owner. The walls are of double thickness, every room being shut off from the one adjoining, by a space of perhaps a foot, enclosed by two solid walls, so that voices can never be heard in the next room unless a door is open. Judge Lee is highly respected as an honorable man, true to his principles, warm in his friendships, and genial and kindly in manner. In my

[1] This house was occupied subsequently, also, by Madame Riedesel, and is now the property of Mr. John Brewster. — ED.

childish days I used occasionally to visit at his house, and my eyes always found a world of pleasure to explore in the pleasant rooms hung with landscape paper and well stocked with pictures and ornaments, while the wide window seats afforded a resting-place for me to view the surrounding landscape. I remember with especial pleasure a complete set of linen coverings on the furniture and bed in an upper chamber. The gay figures of birds perched upon trees scarcely larger than themselves, the tempting strawberries corresponding in size to the plants by their side, the dogs and deer, and animals I could find no names for, all worked in gorgeous colored worsteds by the aristocratic fingers of Mrs. Lee, these had a peculiar fascination for me.

Next in our ride we come to a large square mansion, formerly the residence of Mr. George Ruggles, which he left in affright after the war began, and on the opposite side of the road stands the house of Lieutenant-Governor Oliver.[1] We will drive up the broad carriage road and alight at the door. This lordly house is surrounded by a grove of noble elms and pines, and by wide lawns which are growing green with the touch of spring. The interior is in keeping with its outward appearance, grand in proportions, reminding one of the generous and kindly nature of its proprietor. Of course we do not find it as in the days of his ownership, for soldiers' feet have trod its halls and sick men's moans have been heard in its chambers since the departure of our last royal lieutenant-governor. Its hospital uses interfered in some measure, of course, with the elegance of its former state. Governor Oliver was appointed successor to Andrew Oliver the unpopular lieutenant-governor who died in March, 1774, and was also president of the council of Massachusetts, but owing to the troublous times and the manner of his appointment as councillor, became so obnoxious to the people that he was forced to resign September 2d, only a few months after entering upon his duties. A mob surrounded his house and presented him with a written document to which they demanded his signature. Persistently he refused, until their fury became such as to endanger his life and the safety of his family. Then he took the paper, and hastily casting his eyes over its contents, which was a formal resignation of his office, he wrote these words : " My house at Cambridge being surrounded by four thousand people, in compliance with their commands, I sign my name, Thomas Oliver." Immediately after this he left his Cambridge home and never returned. The field opposite Colonel Oliver's and Captain Ruggles's estates is used as a burying-ground for the brave men who had been wounded at Bunker Hill and died in the two neighboring houses. We are now in Watertown. Shall we ride still further or shall Tony turn the horse and drive us home again ? You have seen a good deal of our beautiful town by proxy, and I hope it will not be long be-

---

[1] This estate is now the property of Mr. James Russell Lowell. The house was built by Thomas Oliver, between 1763 and 1767. — ED.

fore you see it with your own eyes. Till then, dearest Esther, believe me, with tenderest affection, your very sincere friend,

DOROTHY DUDLEY.

May 9th. — Dr. Church and his friends have sent a petition to Congress for his release from prison, as his health is suffering. The plea is granted, only on condition that he give his word of honor, with sureties of one thousand pounds, that he will not hold any correspondence with the enemy, and that he be brought to Massachusetts to be in charge of the council of this Colony, and not privileged to go out of its limits without a license.

May 17th. — Fast day, by resolution of Congress. Dr. Appleton preached to us this morning a faithful and patriotic sermon. This evening news comes to us of the capture of one of the British transport ships, *Hope*, (isn't it a misnomer?) by the schooner *Franklin*, commanded by Captain James Mugford of Marblehead. It is a prize worth capturing, containing, as it does, fifteen hundred barrels of powder and other valuable loading, and one thousand carbines.

May 20th. — Yesterday there was a sharp battle in the harbor. The British navy, it seems, will not let *Hope* go without a struggle, and last night about thirteen boats from the men-of-war at Nantasket attacked the *Franklin*, and a small privateer, the *Lady Washington*, anchored near, and there was determined fighting on both sides. Two of the enemy's boats were sunk. Brave Captain Mugford was mortally wounded, but still kept up the courage of his men, crying: "Do not give up the ship, — you will beat them off!" They did beat them off, but the noble captain did not live to see the victory. He was the only man killed on our side. To-day they have carried him to his home in Marblehead, to bury him.

May 28th. — Massachusetts has taken the lead in the movement for independence. There is scarcely anything else spoken of. The Provincial Congress, May 10th, acted in reference to it, and our town held a meeting the other day, the record of which my friend, the town clerk, has copied for me.

"CAMBRIDGE, *May 27th* 1776.

"At a meeting of the Freeholders & other Inhabitants of the Town Legally warned to Instruct & advise their Representatives, whether, that if the Honb[l] Congress should for the Safety of the Colonies declare them Independent of the Kingdom of Great Britain, they the said Inhabitants will solemnly engage with their Lives & Fortunes to Support them in the Measure.

"Cap[t] Ebenezer Stedman chosen Moderator.

"Unanimously voted, Whereas in the late House of Representatives of this Colony May 10th 1776, it was Resolved as the Opinion of that House, that the Inhabitants of each Town in this Colony ought in full Town Meeting warned for that purpose, to advise the Person or Persons who shall be chosen to Represent them in the next General Court, whether that if the Honorable Congress should for the Safety of the said Colonies declare them Independant of the Kingdom of great Britain, they the said Inhabitants will solemnly engage with their Lives & Fortunes to support them in the measure.

"We the Inhabitants of the Town of Cambridge in full Town meeting assembled, & warned for the Purpose aforesaid, do solemnly engage with our Lives & Fortunes to support them in the Measure."

June 13*th.* — When are we to be rid of the British fleet? Our harbor has given space to them surely long enough. They say there are several hundred Highlanders, on board the eight ships, two brigs, and one schooner, which compose it. General Benjamin Lincoln has a plan for driving them

FIRST STOUGHTON HALL. (TAKEN DOWN 1780.)

off to sea, and to-day orders were given to the people of Boston, to build fortifications in the lower harbor, in anticipation of any trouble. Troops have embarked for Pettick's Island and Hull, about six hundred men at each place, and bodies of militia and artillery are stationed on Moon Island, at Hoff's Neck, and at Point Alderton. On Long Island, also, a detachment is posted, with two eighteen pound guns, and a thirteen inch mortar. Colonel Whitcomb commands the whole.

June 14*th.* — This morning the fleet was fired upon from Long Island, and returned the fire with vigor. At last one of the ships was pierced with a shot, and the Commodore gave orders to put to sea, which was done immediately, after first blowing up the light-house. Just two years to-day since Boston harbor was closed by British tyranny to American vessels! The anniversary is celebrated by the expulsion of his Majesty's ships from the same bay, which will not hold them again we hope, unless as prisoners of war.

June 17th. — At last the students have come back, after a banishment of fourteen months from their college halls. It seems like old times to see the college yard dotted with familiar forms, wending their way, books in hand, from Massachusetts to Harvard, from Hollis to Stoughton and Holden, and promenading through the grounds which our brave Bluecoats so lately trod with martial step and soldiers' bearing. Their home in Concord was without many of the comforts and conveniences they had come to consider necessary to successful study. No halls; but few books, or maps, or apparatus, to aid them up the hill of learning; no wonder that the privilege of return to the college is hailed with joy. It is a time of general thanksgiving, and yesterday our honored President preached a sermon full of gratitude to our Heavenly Father, who has so kindly cared for the interests of Harvard, and brought it back again to its ancient home. Good old Dr. Watts's hymn on God's condescension to human affairs, never seemed more appropriate than when it rung out to the music of manly voices, through the Sabbath stillness, waking an answering song of praise from the birds, the winged worshippers in God's outer temple of nature : —

" 1 Up to the Lord that reigns on high,
 And views the nations from afar,
 Let everlasting praises fly,
 And tell how large His bounties are.

2 [He that can shake the worlds He made,
 Or with His word or with His rod,
 His goodness, how amazing great!
 And what a condescending God!]

3 [God that must stoop to view the skies,
 And bow to see what angels do,
 Down to the earth He casts His eyes,
 And bends His footsteps downwards too.]

4 He overrules all mortal things,
 And manages our mean affairs;
 On humble souls the King of Kings
 Bestows His counsels and His cares.

5 Our sorrows and our tears we pour,
 Into the bosom of our God;
 He hears us in the mournful hour,
 And helps to bear the heavy load.

6 In vain might lofty princes try
 Such condescension to perform!
 For worms were never raised so high
 Above their meanest fellow-worm.

7 Oh! could our thankful hearts devise
 A tribute equal to Thy grace,
 To the third heav'n our songs should rise,
 And teach the golden harps Thy praise."

An Anniversary.

Most of the students were present, and the meeting-house was full. To-day is the first anniversary of the battle which cost us the loss of General Joseph Warren, of fragrant memory, and with him many soldiers brave and loyal to their country. These anniversaries are sad, and yet there is an element of thankfulness in our feelings, as we remember the honors so gloriously earned by our noble men, and the proofs given to all the world, of their patriotism and unflinching courage.

July 3d. — Another anniversary, not of a contest of arms, but of an occasion of very great importance to the country. Just one year to-day since General Washington, under the superb elm which we love to call by his name, formally assumed the command of our immense body of armed men. An army it could scarcely be called, it was so sadly in need of all the requisite implements of war, and the discipline which his firm hand and wise head brought to the disorderly mass. At this distance of time we can more easily understand the dreadful difficulties he had to surmount to preserve the appearance of a well-equipped army in the eyes of the Redcoats under Sir William Howe. For eleven months they stood in awe of our guns, and would not venture forth from beleaguered Boston to attack the surrounding strongholds. Their final evacuation on St. Patrick's Day was regarded with astonishment in England, where the indomitable perseverance and unequalled skill of our great general are not understood. Mr. Hancock's letter to General Washington, on that occasion, expressed the universal feeling of gratitude and admiration extended to him : —

"Philadelphia, *2d April*, 1776.

"Sir, — It gives me the most sensible pleasure to convey to you, by order of Congress, the only tribute which a free people will ever consent to pay, the tribute of thanks and gratitude to their friends and benefactors. The disinterested and patriotic principles, which led you to the field, have also led you to glory ; and it affords no little consolation to your countrymen to reflect, that, as a peculiar greatness of mind induced you to decline any compensation for serving them, except the pleasure of promoting their happiness, they may without your permission, bestow upon you the largest share of their affections and esteem.

" Those pages in the annals of America will record your title to a conspicuous place in the temple of fame, which shall inform posterity, that, under your direction, an undisciplined band of husbandmen in the course of a few months became soldiers ; and that the desolation meditated against the country by a brave army of veterans, commanded by the most experienced generals, but employed by bad men in the worst of causes, was, by the fortitude of your troops, and the address of their officers, next to the kind interposition of Providence, confined for near a year within such narrow limits, as scarcely to admit more room than was necessary for the encampments and fortifications they lately abandoned. Accept, therefore,

Sir, the thanks of the United Colonies, unanimously declared by their delegates to be due to you, and the brave officers and troops under your command ; and be pleased to communicate to them this distinguished mark of the approbation of their country. The Congress have ordered a golden medal, adapted to the occasion, to be struck, and when finished, to be presented to you.

"I have the honor to be, with every sentiment of esteem, Sir, your most obedient and very humble servant,

"JOHN HANCOCK, *President*."

July 5th. — My friend Esther Livingstone has sent me copies of two letters from Mr. Edmund Quincy,[1] to his daughter Katy. Esther has become well acquainted with Miss Quincy, and knowing the interest they would possess for me, begged to be allowed to copy the letters for my pleasure.

"LANCASTER, *May 27th*, 1776."

"TO MISS KATY QUINCY.

"*Dear Child.* — As you are called in the Providence of God, to take so long a journey as from hence to Philad^a at ye request of Mr. Hancock & y^r Sister, to accomp^y & be a comfort to her who by ye same providence has been conducted thither & there it's probable she may have her residence, yet for some considerable time, if ye present civil war should by *Him* be permitted to continue to another year. I am to wish you a safe & comfortable journey, & that it may prove advantageous to y^r health, & that ye may meet y^r B^r & S^r in an equal enjoyment of theirs.

"The parent country and these united provinces are doubtless for very wise reasons & ends suffered to be involved in one common calamity, that of a civil & bloody war. Yet we have great cause of thankfulness in this province especially in wh ye war began: (1775 Apr. 19) having on ye 17th of March last been kindly delivered (nearly without bloodshed) from so large a no of troops collected in our *Capital* wh, as you know, I have always viewed as a merciful token of a General hopeless Evacuation of ye most atrocious & savage as well as impolitic undertaking to subjugate 3 mill^s of people, distant 3200 geographic miles, united in 13 colonies ; nor is anything similar to be found in either antient or modern History. Those who may live to see ye close of ye present century * * * * will doubtless discern that in infinite wisdom & goodness God has permitted ye present evil day to overtake us. * * * * Much division is unhappily occasioned among Friends, & some large soci-

---

[1] Edmund Quincy was graduated at Harvard in 1732. He then went into business with his brother Josiah, and his brother-in-law Edmund Jackson (the husband of "Dorothy Q."). They were very prosperous, having extensive European business relations, and, in 1750, when they dissolved partnership, divided upwards of $300,000, a large fortune in those days. Josiah Quincy retired to Braintree, and retained his property and his portion of the paternal estate ; but Edmund entered business again, with his sons Edmund and Henry. The new firm was unfortunate, and, after 1759, the writer of the letter in the text lived in Boston in comparatively restricted circumstances until his death. During the siege he retired to Lancaster. His daughters were remarkable for their beauty. — ED.

eties very much thro' the lust of pride & thirst of power over their Brethren wh. will appear on both sides of the water, to have ye original of ye present strange event. Probably as many of this class of aspiring men may have sprung from this province as any other & perhaps more as it is certain *One* among those who have tho't it best to exile themselves from their native land, has been ever charg'd with acting such a part, thro' the whole of his publ admon & upon every private occasion as finally to fix ye foregoing character upon him, especially among those who have been cotemporary in govern^t (who have been numerous he beginning very young) W^t the fatal issue may prove to those who have listed under his Banners, none can tell — this is certain and awful that their Salvation, if obtained, must arise from ye destruction of ye Liberty of America & probably of mankind. We may discern some things in ye present scene of things, but we are doomed to blindness as to the future — we have nevertheless our several parts to act & those especially in Government, in these days of trial are indisputably called in their several departments to provide such means of resistance as may be judged adequate to that defence we are under the necessity of making. Still may our confidence be placed on *him* whose arm alone can and will save us, as he has often done our fathers in this land, w^m little better than a howling desert. They were never indeed called to a similar trial but they were more than once in danger of total excision from ye savage nations of the wilderness ; yet ye wisest of our predecessors, never surely formed an Idea of ye possibillity of any B. Europeans making assault upon their best friends in so savage a manner, no way very dissimilar (except in y^e *Naval* armament) to the victories of Fire & Sword, wch our fathers sufferd from their Indian enemies, more cruel than ye beasts of prey. I have often pictured to you what I thought of ye original of ye remarkable change in ye Governors of ye B. Nation touching ye subordinates rule among ye cols. I suspect they will very soon have reason to tremble at ye approaching breach wth France & Spain. It must prove ye dangerous war G. B. has been for more than a century past involved in. The patriotic D of Richmond & good B. of St. Asaph have wrote en^o to confirm every sensible man in the same sentiments wh they have very freely publ^d in ye 1774.

"My devout wish is that ye Brit. people may soon see ye Err^s of their present Rulers, & that God may have mercy upon them and early prevent their final ruin — wh certainly awaits them unless saved by repentance & reform^a —

"I w'd have y^u give me (und^r Mr. H & Frank) ye earliest notice of y^r safe arrival at P. and of his & y^r sister's state of health: also ch^rg Dr. Y. home wth his neglect of corresp^ce — if ye effect of an extensive practise it will be some excuse. Dont forget ye pamphlet called ye 2^d appeal to Jus^tce of Jany 10, last — of wh. we had some clauses in ye Boston paper. — if at Ph^a upon return of Mr. Bant send me anything wh is worth sending, & Desire Dr. Young to comply with his promise of a copy ye City new government — My best wishes attend you in y^r present long journey & hope under Mr. Bants convoy you'll arrive in at least a comfortable manner. If y^u should consent to be inoculated I hope you'll be attended by a skilful Physitian : — at ye same time you'll remember to fix y^r chief trust in ye G^t Physitian of soul & body. To whose kind providence I commend you & rem^n Dr Child y^r very aff^t Fa & Friend."

"LANCASTER *June 10th* 1776.

"*Dear Dr Katy.* Since y^r departure we've no certain advices from our army in Canada, only that there has been a very important battle between them and Carlton's troops & that in gen^l our army obtains a victory — possibly the particulars have reached P. ere this will come to hand. We are not a little concerned least Burgoine may have arrived with his troops, time eno. to prevent our gaining ye fortress of Q. however we must submit to ye determin^a of a wise provid^ce, not doubting the issue will be in our favor. We hear from Halifax that sickness prevails among the troops there. By a ship there fro G. B. there comes advice that ye Fleet, sail'd for America had met with such bad weather, as to disperse almost ye whole, some of wh. had put into Lisbon, others into France & some ret^d. By wch disaster possibly a much less formidable force will arrive safe than has been feared by some & wished for by others — it is certain, we have as yet no certain acc^t of ye arrival of any large force at H^x nevertheless the fortifications are going forward at Boston wth vigour, & its expected their strength will be very sufficient to oppose an entrance into ye upper harbour, sh^d an attempt be made by Adm^l Howe ; but I rather think that his grand effort will be agnst N. Y^r not by nature so capable of defense as Boston, w^h his B^r ab^t 3 mo. ago so unexpectedly and shamelessly evacuated, ye advise of wh., we may expect to hear, has been more surprising to ye adm^l (if arrived) than anything he had before met with : as it must have in a great measure disconcerted ye ministerial plan of operation ; & should some more of the most important store-ships of Parker's Fleet be lost, or delayed by their repairs in any port wh. they might have made after ye Storm, the summer may prove too short for ye Execution of their *infernal* design, for it appears to me it will deserve no softer Epithet : and I think I know the source, & am very little at a loss, as to ye general issue of the present nonpareil controversy — The Britons tell us, tho' wth singular impropriety & very little truth, that they have with great care & expenses, settled, nourished & defended these N^o American Col^s from their infancy & therefore that they are chargeable wth ye blackest ingratitude as well as ye greatest injustice in ye resistance wh. they have dared to make ag^t ye sovereign authority of ye B. empire. Administration have, from the first forming of their plan of subjug^n, flatter^d thems. that ye Col^s would not unite in an opposition, being, as I apprehend, judicially blinded fro. ye beginning, even so far as to assure thems. that 13 considerable provinces under a free Gov^t w^d be frighted into an immediate compliance wth their demand — upon ye sight of

Independence at Last.

a Comparatively Small no. of troops parading in ye Streets of Boston, & a few large ships in its harbour, ready to cooperate wth the same upon opposition. To this egregious blunder of ye B. Govt ye present safety of these A. Cols, has been, & is, greatly owing, inasmuch as it has, for several years, prevented ye ministry fr. applyg to Pt for such a formidable force as they threaten this year to bring against us. We hear of sundry prize ships, sent into several parts since you left us — 2 sugar ships from Jamaica, one 450 tons — 30 Gentn & ladies passengers — wth 20000 dollars on brd besides a valuable Cargo — ye passengers by agreemt were landed at Providence — this morning advise of a Scotch ship wth a no of highlanders & others near about 140 wth Cargo brot into Salem as soldiers — they are best under our command. Let me know if any good manufacrs are hopefully rising in or near P. The present Scarcity of B. Commods is & will prove of vast advante to ye whole Amn Community — tho' a fatal stab to ye B. commerce. To prevent ye latter, I presume, admtion has made an argumt of ye apparent danger to persuade B. merchants & manufacrs to lend them aid to ye present grand preparations, with many promises of compensa for all their losses out of ye Amcan forfeited estates. One wd almost think that *Reason* as well as virtue had taken its flight fr the most important ranks of B. Subjects."

July 19*th.* — Independence is declared at last! The glorious document which proclaims our Colonies to be free and independent States, has been read from the balcony of the State House and in Faneuil Hall, and greeted with cheers of welcome from thousands of patriotic throats. The thought of independence has been a familiar one for many months, and the fiery enthusiasm which now flames forth from all quarters tells of the universal joy of the nation. The seventh day of June Mr. Richard Henry Lee of Virginia made a motion in Congress, that "these United Colonies are and of right ought to be free and independent States," and proposed that they dissolve all connection with the mother country. The question was debated vigorously and eloquently, and on the eleventh of June a committee, consisting of Thomas Jefferson of Virginia, John Adams of our own Colony, Benjamin Franklin of Pennsylvania, Roger Sherman of Connecticut, and Robert R. Livingston of New York, was appointed to draft a Declaration of Independence. Each member of the committee drew up such a paper as expressed his 'own views and feelings, and then the five met for consultation. Mr. Jefferson's paper was read first, and so entirely met the approval of the others, that it was unanimously adopted as being in every way superior to their own. This was reported to Congress, and after being discussed several days and slightly altered, was agreed to on the fourth day of July. The streets of Philadelphia, on that day, were filled with eager crowds, waiting to know the decision of Congress. The bell-ringer of the State House stood at his post in the steeple, from the early morning, that he might be prompt to announce to the people that their independence was formally declared. His little boy was stationed where he could get the earliest news of the event and at last, as the old man grew impatient at the long delay, the boyish voice rung through the air: "Ring! Ring, Father! Ring!" And then the bells sent forth a triumphant peal which was answered by shouts of joy from the excited multitude. The declaration thus concludes: "We, therefore, the representatives of the United States of America in General Congress assembled, appealing to the Supreme Judge of the World for the rectitude of our intentions, do, in the name, and by the authority of the good people of these Colonies, solemnly publish and declare, That these United Colonies are, and of right ought to be, *Free and Independent States;* that they are absolved from all allegiance to the British crown, and that all political connection between them and the state of Great Britian, is, and ought to be, totally dissolved; and that, as Free and Independent States, they have full power to levy war, conclude peace, contract alliances, establish commerce, and to do all other acts and things which Independent States may of right do. And for the support of this declaration, with a *firm* reliance on the protection of *Divine Providence*, we mutually pledge to each other our lives, our fortunes, and our sacred honor."

Though this declaration was agreed to on the fourth, the resolution adopting it was passed on the second day of July, and Mr. John Adams, writing on the day after that memorable event, says: "The second day of July, 1776, will be the most memorable epocha in the history of America; to be celebrated by succeeding generations as the great anniversary festival, commemorated as the day of deliverance by solemn acts of devotion to God Almighty, from one end of the continent to the other, from this time forward forevermore. I am well aware of the toil, and blood, and treasure that it will cost us to maintain this declaration, and support and defend these States; yet through all the gloom, I can see the rays of light and glory; that the end is worth all the means; that posterity will triumph in that day's transaction, even though we should rue it, which I trust in God we shall not."

[The Editor reluctantly closes his extracts from Miss Dudley's Diary at this point. It would be interesting to read her animadversions upon the succeeding events, but they would frequently take us away from Cambridge, which, as she has remarked, was very quiet after the evacuation of Boston.

The extracts already given subserve the purposes of this volume, and are also unconscious witnesses to the firm and enthusiastic patriotism of the writer, as well as to her remarkable ability as a gatherer and recorder of current news at a period when the public press was not the all-pervading power that it now is.]

THE GUESTS AT HEAD-QUARTERS.

BY H. E. SCUDDER.

THE great square house which was provided for Washington's head-quarters in Cambridge, had seen a generous hospitality displayed, no doubt, when Mr. John Vassall occupied it and looked out over the broad acres attached to it, and noted the half dozen similar mansions scattered along the Watertown Road, that held his Tory neighbors. But the Virginian who took possession brought with him traditions of ample living and social habits which were re-enforced by the demands made upon the Commander-in-chief of the Continental army. Washington was a soldier, and a man, besides, of self-restraint. His moderation was seen in his diet, which was extremely simple, sometimes nothing, we are told, but baked apples or berries with cream and milk; and in his early and regular hours. As the central figure, however, in the American army, and representative of the cause which brought soldiers and civilians to Cambridge, he gathered about him, at his head-quarters, the officers of the army and the prominent visitors who for public or personal reasons made their way to the camp. The Provincial Congress enabled him to maintain a style of living which comported with his position, and his table was the social centre of the camp. Some of his officers dined with him every day. Let us see who they were that became familiar with the halls of this historic house.

Major-General Charles Lee was the most conspicuous of the military men toward whom the young country, anxious for heroes, looked with admiration. His romantic career as a soldier of fortune, his ready defence of the American cause, when other men of patriotic principle were more cautious, and his reputation for personal courage, gave him at once a strong hold upon the popular mind. Indeed, he cut a dashing figure beside the dignified, reserved Washington. He has been well described in his personal appearance as "a tall man, lank and thin, with a huge nose, a satirical mouth, and restless eyes, who sat his horse as if he had often ridden at fox-hunts in England, and wore his uniform with a cynical disregard of common opinion."[1] Seen near at hand, this restless, ambitious man piqued his comrades and friends by his apparently indifferent, contemptuous ways. He was always attended by a great dog, Spada by name, perhaps brought

[1] Greene's *Life of Nathanael Greene*, vol. i. p. 100.

with him from Portugal, that shared his quarters in Hobgoblin Hall, went with him to dinner parties, and was formally presented to his guests and friends. Two years later, when General Lee was a prisoner, his dog was sent down the lines by General Greene under passport, and passes out of history just as Lee himself enters the shadow of a terrible reproach.

Of all the officers who then sat at Washington's table, Nathanael Greene was the one whose laurels have remained the most unfaded. This sturdy Quaker bred anchor-smith, who by slow but sure degrees had been welding his Quaker integrity and business faculty into sinewy completeness, now at the time of need was found with a steady brain and ready hand, slipping off easily the civilian and letting the soldier and sagacious general come forth. Washington's right hand man in the hard struggle to come, that was to witness cabals and intrigues as well as open enmities, it is impossible but that the great general should have looked upon this New England man as one of the most welcome at his table.

The soldiers' favorite, General Israel Putnam, was also one of Washington's guests. No doubt this hot-headed, blustering, but brave officer brought other than the politest manners to the table of the Virginian gentleman, but Washington, with his cool, clear judgment of men, was not one to be governed in his tastes by the presence or lack of elegant manners. General Putnam brought to the military society an intrepid courage, a readiness of invention, and a *bonhomie* which must have rendered him an important element. One scene laid at the head-quarters is given, when Old Put dashes up to the gateway, bearing behind his saddle the woman to whom Church had intrusted his treacherous letter, and drags her, terrified, up the broad pathway to the door.

Major Thomas Mifflin, afterwards general, now upon Washington's staff, and residing in the old Brattle House facing the lane that led to Harvard Square, must have been a constant visitor. Brave and eloquent, he had a presence and manner which charmed all about him. His wife, in delicate health, was with him, but this did not prevent him from being eagerly sought by all the ladies in society, who sang his praise with hearty unanimity. It was he who, raised to the rank of colonel and quartermaster-general, was called to the council for determining the day when Dorchester Heights should be taken possession of, and made the suggestion, so quickly taken up, that the night of the 4th of March should be chosen, since then, if a battle were fought on the 5th, the memory of the "Massacre" would give a rallying cry to the soldiers.

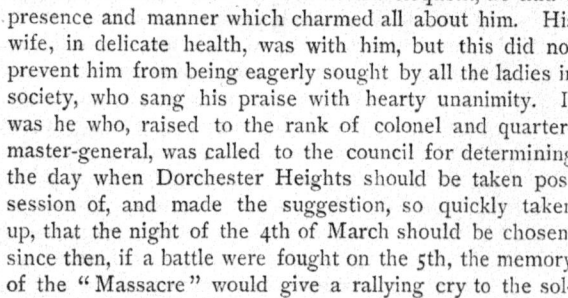

THE BRATTLE ARMS.

Closer to Washington's person was the accomplished Joseph Reed, his secretary and dear friend, who wrote so freely and easily, and between whom and Washington there subsisted so charming a relation, leading the reserved general to write almost boyishly to the junior soldier. His answer to Governor Johnstone's temptation — "I am not worth purchasing; but such as I am the King of Great Britain is not rich enough to do it," was the instantaneous and scornful message of a man of the highest honor.

It was in July when Washington took possession of the Vassall house, and in November he was joined by Mrs. Washington, who made the soldiers' quarters a home, and received there the officers' wives, who had joined their husbands when it was evident that the siege was to be a winter one. Mrs. Greene was one of these, and out of the friendship that there sprang up came the names of George and Martha Washington given to the two children of General Greene and his wife. Mrs. John Adams also was a visitor, and records in her lively letters the social stir that was known in the Cambridge camp at this period.

But it was not only these who walked the broad pathway to the Vassall house, — officers and officers' wives and neighboring civilians, — but hospitality was extended to the public men of the Colony, to the members of the Committee of Safety who visited the General, and of the Provincial Congress, sitting hard by in Watertown. The most noted company, however, that sat at Washington's table, was when in October a committee of Congress, consisting of Benjamin Franklin, Thomas Lynch of Carolina, and Colonel Harrison of Virginia, arrived to confer with the generals. With these commissioners were present Deputy-Governor Griswold and Judge Nathaniel Wales from Connecticut, Deputy-Governor Cooke from Rhode Island, James Bowdoin, Colonel Otis, William Sever and Walter Spooner of the Massachusetts Council. The records of this conference have been preserved, and are a matter of history. We have a glimpse of a dinner party given to them, afforded by Dr. Belknap, who was a guest, and who writes : " Lynch, Harrison, and Wales wished to see Boston in flames. Lee told them it was impossible to burn it unless they sent men in with bundles of straw on their backs to do it. He said it could not be done with carcass and hot shot ; and instanced the Isle Royal, in St. Lawrence River, which was fired at in 1760 a long time, with a fine train of artillery, hot shot, and carcasses, without effect." [1]

In this extract Dr. Franklin's voice is not heard. We can imagine that no visitor would attract more attention than this renowned man, who sat and listened to a discussion whether his native town should be destroyed. He was sixty-nine years old at this time, twenty-six years older than the commanding general. He represented the mind which had foreseen the impending conflict years before, and was able now to write to his philosophic friend Priestley : " Enough has happened, one would think, to convince your ministers that the Americans will fight, and that this is a harder nut to crack than they imagine." His buoyant, hopeful nature, and shrewd, worldly wisdom, must have given to General Washington at this time a sense

---

[1] *Life of Dr. Belknap*, p. 96, quoted in Frothingham's *Siege of Boston*, p. 257.

of strength in the council at Philadelphia, and it is not hard to imagine that between the great general and the sagacious statesman there should have passed much deliberation, weighing of men and measures, gauging of the forces in conflict.

The walls of the Vassall House resounded to talk of war and sport and frolic. Often Washington left the table in charge of one of his aids, and retired in accordance with his methodical habits. No one has preserved the record of the jest and story that were tossed back and forth by the eager young officers who were entering upon a war which, in its seven years' detail, was to sober some, and lay some in the grave. The victories of peace, of scholarship, and of letters, have been won because of the conferences there held in the early days of the Revolution. The clank of spur and sword have ceased, but the voices of wisdom and of mirth have never yet died out within those historic walls.

THE BATCHELDER HOUSE, AND ITS OWNERS.

BY MRS. ISABELLA JAMES.

"We have no title-deeds to house or lands;
Owners and occupants of earlier dates
From graves forgotten stretch their dusty hands,
And hold in mortmain still their old estates."
LONGFELLOW.

THE story of a house where many generations have lived and died, can hardly be contained within the brief space allowed in this volume, yet these pages will give in as condensed form as possible some interesting facts connected with one of the most ancient houses of this historic town, if not the very oldest now standing in Cambridge. The dates here given, which will correct some accounts previously printed, have been drawn from deeds and other legal papers by the present owner of the estate, aged ninety-one and a half, who has held and occupied it for thirty-four years.

This ancient house stands on the southwesterly side of the old Watertown Road nearly opposite Mason Street. The first recognition of any highway in the town records of Cambridge is December 2, 1633: "Ordered that no person shall fell any trees within the path that goeth from Watertown to Charlestown." This path [1] is what was afterwards called the King's highway, and until after the Revolution was the only route from Market Square and the colleges to Watertown and the country beyond.

From the early records it appears that this part of Cambridge was called West End, for in the account of the houses and lands of the inhabitants of the town given in at a General Court holden at Boston 6th of 7th mo. A. D. 1642. "Cary Latham.[2] Imprimis, in West End, one dwelling house with outhouses and seven acres of land more or less;" then follow the boundaries on the southeast by Ash Street at that time called the Highway to Windmill Hill,[3] and northeast the highway to Watertown. 20th 5th mo., 1645, Latham conveyed the estate with the same boundaries to Thomas Crosby. At the first settlement of Cambridge, it appears that part of this land facing the Watertown Road was laid off in half-acre lots, one of which was owned and

---

[1] Now Kirkland, Garden, Mason, and Brattle streets.
[2] He removed early to New London, where he was representative in 1664 and 1670. — *Sav. Gen.*
[3] In a grant of land March 2d, to John Benjamin, there is this reservation, "Provided that the Windmill Hill shall be reserved for the town's use and a cartway of two rods wide unto the same."

occupied by Roger Bancroft before 1645, for in that year he bought another adjoining from Robert Parker, a butcher, whose son John graduated at Harvard University, 1661. Evidence of this occupation of the premises two hundred and thirty years ago appeared when Brattle Street was widened in 1871. The excavations made to rebuild the wall revealed heaps of animal bones which for a few hours created quite a sensation in the neighborhood. No record of a deed from Crosby can be found; but Thomas Marrit, one of the early settlers of Cambridge, was in possession of the property in 1663. From his will and inventory it appears that he held a good deal of land in this part of the town, the West End and West fields, and it was probably from his great-grandson Amos [1] that Colonel Vassall, nearly a century later, bought the land that so long bore the name of Vassall. The last clause of Thomas Marrit's will, dated October 15, 1663, is as follows: —

"To the children of my sonne George Bastow I do give and bequeath in full of what I stand engaged to them fifty-two pounds, on payment whereof they shall give my executor a full and final discharge, and for the payment thereof this house and land wherein my sonne John Marrit lives to my friend Roger Bancroft to stand engaged on payment of the debt and legacy. He may sell or dispose of the said House and land as he shall please; finally I do nominate and appoint my sonne John Marrit sole executor to this my last will and Testament." In the inventory that follows the first entry is "The dwelling house and outhouses orchard and upland and meadow and marsh and the Wold adjoining £90 00 00." The seventh "The dwelling house and outhouses that was Roger Bancroft's and eight acres of land £50 00 00." Thomas Marrit died in 1664; and September 21, 1665, John Marrit conveyed to Jonathan Remington "one messuage or tenement in Cambridge containing one dwelling house, outhouses and barns and five acres of land adjoining thereto." From the boundaries given in this deed the lot fronting on the Watertown Road extended from the western line of the present row of old hawthorns and lindens to what is now Ash Street, excepting a half-acre house lot [2] at that corner, and southerly nearly to the marsh.

Ash Street, once called Bath Lane, but previously known as the highway to Windmill Hill, was the northwestern boundary of the palisado which the Court voted in 1632 to erect about "the New-Towne." This protection against the wild inhabitants of the land commenced at Brick Wharf, says Holmes, then called Windmill Hill. About thirty years ago a mound was plainly visible at the corner of Bath Lane, and the back road to Mount Auburn, which was known to the young people of the writer's generation as the Old Fort. When the street was straightened in 1844, and the present proprietor bought a corner of the land and removed his fence, the foundation of this fortification was uncovered revealing a built up wall of stones. The house erected by Abel Stevens in 1874 now occupies the spot.

[1] A grandson, Amos Marrit, is mentioned in his will.
[2] Then the premises of Nathaniel Greene and Richard Eccles.

Governor Belcher.

A year before Jonathan Remington purchased this estate, he had married Martha, daughter of the first Andrew Belcher; in this house it is probable that most of their married life was passed; he was town clerk and treasurer of Cambridge for many years; his son, Judge Remington of the Supreme Court, was eminent in his generation, and the daughter of the latter married Lieutenant-Governor William Ellery of Newport, and became the mother of the signer of the Declaration of Independence bearing that name.

September 22, 1682, Jonathan Remington conveyed to his wife's brother, Andrew Belcher, the same estate for £120. He was the son of the first Andrew who came to Cambridge, and was a shipmaster and merchant of Boston. He was called "an ornament and blessing to his country," for after the swamp fight in King Philip's war, December, 1675, Captain Belcher arrived in Narragansett Bay with provisions, and thus saved the troops from perishing. He held many important offices, and was a councillor from 1702 until his death in 1717. In 1700, he gave a bell to the Cambridge meeting-house, and the town gave the "old bell to the Farmers."[1]

At the death of Captain Belcher, this estate was inherited by his only son, Jonathan,[2] who was royal governor of Massachusetts and New Jersey for twenty-seven years. When, in 1730, he received his first appointment in England, Dr. Isaac Watts addressed to him an adulatory poem, some lines of which are said to be so extravagant as to border on impiety. His arrival at Boston with his commission, was hailed with the greatest joy. All the dignitaries of the town went to escort him from the ship; the military were out in full force, cannons were discharged, the turrets and balconies of the houses were covered with flags and carpets, while the shipping in the harbor displayed all their colors. Twenty-five years before this triumphant entry of Governor

THE BELCHER ARMS.

Belcher into Boston, the newspaper of the day described his marriage to Mary, daughter of Lieutenant-Governor William Partridge of New Hampshire. January 4, 1705–06, he was met at Hampton by several gentlemen from Portsmouth, and was accompanied by them and others who attended him, and arrived the same night in order to celebrate his marriage on the 8th, "but at the motion of the gentlemen that accompanied him," the marriage took place "the same night as he came off the journey in his boots. The wedding was celebrated on the Tuesday following (January 8th), when there was a noble and splendid entertainment for the guests." Why this unseemly haste,

---
[1] Cambridge Farms, now Lexington.
[2] For much of the following account of Governor Belcher, I am indebted to the MSS. of Rev. J. L. Sibley, librarian of Harvard University.

the reporter of that day does not inform us; or why the ceremony should have taken place on *Friday* evening, after a long day's journey from Hampton on horseback,[1] in snowy if not muddy boots. We see how our modern telegram might have been useful here in notifying expectant Boston friends that the marriage had taken place four days earlier than had been anticipated. The occasion was "honored with the discharge of the great guns of the fort;" and the same day, it being the one which had been "designed for the marriage, several great guns were discharged at his father, Captain Andrew Belcher, Esq.'s Wharffe, and aboard several ships" at Boston. Under January 23, 1704-05, Sewall writes, "Mr. Jonathan Belcher and his bride dine at Lieutenant-Governor Usher's. Came to town at six o'clock — about twenty horsemen, three coaches and many slays."[2] The grandeur of the bridal occasion was only equalled by Mrs. Belcher's funeral, in 1736, at which it is related one thousand pairs of gloves were given away.

Governor Belcher took a deep interest in the colleges, first of Massachusetts and afterwards of New Jersey. His reply to the clergy on his Sunday at Boston in 1730, bore testimony to his attachment to his Alma Mater. He first met its officers 9th September, 1730, the day of the assembly at Cambridge of a prorogued legislature. He was "guarded into town by a military troop, then waited on by two foot companies." In his speech to the General Court he puts them "in mind of the happiness peculiar to this Province, in the early care our Fathers took for a liberal and pious Education of their Posterity by founding of a College," and assures them he "shall gladly embrace every opportunity they'l put in" his "power of nourishing that seminary of Rilegion and Learning." When he "had done with ye Court for ye forenoon and been a while at Mr. [tutor] Flynt's chamber ye Bell tolled, ye scholars assembled in ye Hall, his Excellency & ye Corporation went in, Mr. Holly made a Latin oration, his Excellency made a very handsome Answer in Latin. This done his Excellency, his Majestie's Council, ye Corporation, Tutors, Professors, with sundry Gentlemen dined in the Library; ye Masters at College were not invited 'twas feared there would not be room for them."

In a speech to the legislature, 16th December, 1730, he says, "When you consider what a diffusive Blessing the College has been to this Country, in its Learning and Religion, and how much all the Estates among you have been rais'd in their Value, and that while other Plantations are oblig'd to send their sons abroad for Education at a great expence, and often to ruin of their Morals, we reap that advantage at home; I say I hope these things

---

[1] It may be possible, but hardly probable, that this journey was performed in sleighs.

[2] "The arms of the United States, viz., 'Pales of thirteen argent and gules, a chief azure,' bear a stronger resemblance to the arms of Belcher than they do to those of Washington. The colors indeed are different, and the number of pales is doubled, yet the principle of the two coats is identical. The Washington arms are as different as possible, having bars instead of pales, and, although our national flag may be founded on the Washington arms, our national seal is not."—*Hist. and Gen. Reg.* vol. xxvii. p. 244.

will make you ready on all occasions to nourish and cherish that society. And what I would particularly point at is the Complaint of the sons of the prophets that they are straitned for room I am told that Stoughton College is gone much to decay, and not without danger of falling I should be therefore glad that a committee of this Court might be chosen to view it and report what may be proper to be done for the better accommodation of the students there."

Governor Belcher desired that his remains should be taken from New Jersey, where he died, to Cambridge, and interred by the side of his dear friend and cousin, Judge Remington. A tomb near the gateway of the graveyard holds the ashes of these eminent men, but the monument ordered to be erected over them was never put up. The estate, held by Remington for seventeen years, and by the Belchers for thirty-seven years, united as they were by the closest ties of blood and friendship, may well be said to have remained in one family for over half a century.

December 1, 1719, Jonathan Belcher conveyed six acres of land with the " dwelling house, barns, outhouses, edifices, fences &c.," to John Frizzle, for £220. He was an eminent merchant of Boston, living at the North End, where Frizzle's Corner, in Garden Street between North and Fleet streets, long commemorated his name. In 1719, he gave to the new North Church a bell, which, though of small size and disagreeable sound, was used until 1802, when the old meeting-house was taken down, and the bell sold to the town of Charlton, Worcester County. Mr. Frizzle died 1723, and Dr. Cotton Mather preached his funeral sermon ; nothing is to be learned from it, says Drake, except that he was an honorable merchant. His widow, Dorothy Frizzle, married Mr. Saltonstall, and died in 1733, leaving £200 to the poor of Boston, and £20 to be laid out in Bibles and Testaments, to be distributed among poor children. The estate was inherited by John Frizzle, Jr., who did not long survive his mother, as his widow Mercy conveyed, July 26, 1736, to John Vassall, "a certain messauge or tenement containing by estimation six acres of land with a dwelling house, barn, and outhouses, thereon standing," for £1,000. When the elder Frizzle purchased the property in 1719, an ounce of silver was worth 12s. in 1736 it was worth 27s. Some antiquarians think that the Frizzles built an entirely new house upon the land, but there is no evidence that the original house was destroyed, though if part of it was left standing, it was much enlarged, altered, and modernized ! It is evident to the present occupants that the eastern part of the house was added about this period ; the original foundation can be seen in the cellar, excluding that portion. The rooms are higher studded in the new part, and the woodwork more elaborate, but the chimneys are laid in clay, which is said to denote the period before the introduction of lime. It will be observed that in each deed nearly the same words are used to describe the estate as in that of 1665, " dwelling-house, out-houses, and barns," which prove that it was then a building of some pretensions. From careful data gathered by the present occupants, the oldest part of the house is the western end, which once consisted of the entry and three rooms on the lower floor; the one on the left of the entrance was a small sitting-room, with two windows looking on the King's highway, while the window on the left of the door facing the paved court, lighted a pantry with oaken dressers, and a broad oak shelf stretched across the window-sill for a punch-bowl, from whence many a stirrup-cup was doubtless drunk.

Over the fire-place in this sitting-room was a panel, which opened outwards, the depth of the chimney being sufficient to conceal a man, as well as papers and treasure. Within the remembrance of the writer, this fireplace and panel were taken out, when pantry and sitting-room were thrown into one. In the early times the kitchen was on the right of the entrance hall, and only of one story. In 1842, when the plastering of the chamber over it had to be renewed, the old weather boarding was exposed, showing that for a long series of years it had been acted upon by the stern winters and hot summers of a New England climate, unprotected by shingles, clapboard, or paint. The size of the kitchen chimney now encased in the wall, recalls the times when ox-teams were necessary to draw the logs for the fire; it is eight feet long and eight deep. The house, though of wood, is filled in with brick, and last year, in cutting a door between two rooms, a well laid brick partition wall had to be penetrated, where the carpenter expected to find only a thin layer of lath and plaster. At what date the third room on the floor, the parlor, was enlarged, we have no means of knowing. Nearly fifty years ago, the house presented a more venerable appearance than now: it was rough cast, and from age had sunk almost below the level of the road; it was raised up, and a new layer of dressed stone put under it; over a foot of earth now covers a handsome pavement of beach pebbles, on the east and south sides of the house; and the southwestern wing containing the kitchen and offices, which were not raised with the main building, remains to prove the level of the old house.

We now return to 1736, when the estate passed into the possession of Colonel John Vassall, to whom the house has often been said to owe its origin. So much has been written and printed about the Vassalls, that it need only be stated here, that they were an important family in Old England, and early connected with the settlement of New England. They owned large plantations in the British West Indies, and several fine estates in Boston and its vicinity. It may be well to correct here a false impression that has prevailed, that some of the Vassall family had held the lands known by their name, from the early settlement of Cambridge; but the first of their property here was this purchased of Mrs. Frizzle in 1736, and it was not until some years after John Vassall had *sold* it to his brother, that he bought the land[1] afterwards known as the Cragie estate. The entire period when the various members of the family resided in this town, was

---

[1] A part of it, from Amos Marrit.

less than forty years, but the impression they made upon the age yet survives.

Colonel John Vassall, one of seventeen children, married Elizabeth, daughter of Lieutenant-Governor Phipps ; her three sisters [1] married gentlemen of distinction, who also lived in Cambridge, and her only brother resided in the old house, still standing in Bow and Arrow streets, sometimes called the Winthrop House. It was no doubt the family interest of the Phippses in this town that induced Colonel Vassall to settle here. Mrs. Vassall died in 1739, and it was this breaking up of his family that caused him to sell the property to his brother, then just about marrying a rich lady, also from the West Indies.

In 1741, Colonel Vassall *sold*[2] to his "brother Henry, now residing in Boston, late of the Island of Jamaica, planter, seven acres of land, be it more or less, with a dwelling-house, barn, and out-houses thereon standing ; " then follow the boundaries, which include the acre and a half now the western end of the estate on Brattle Street, for which Colonel Vassall had obtained, in 1737, a quitclaim deed from the heirs of Luxford Patten, for £100. The planting of the row of hawthorns and lindens must be due to an older owner than the Vassalls, as it marks the line between their estate and the Luxfords, and was doubtless to shield the Frizzles from neighboring eyes, for a house once stood on that lot. When one of the lindens died, twenty-four years ago, more than one hundred rings were counted in its trunk. With the house and land, Colonel Vassal sold " the furniture, chariot, four-wheeled chaise, two bay stone horses, and two black geldings," for £8,050. At this period an ounce of silver was worth 25s., and it was a season of great commercial prosperity. It is stated that the accounts of the wealth of Boston and the vicinity carried home by the English officers after the taking of Louisburg in 1745, was the cause of the taxation of the Colonies which resulted in their loss to the British crown.

In 1742, soon after the purchase of the house and furniture, Major Henry Vassall married Penelope, daughter of Isaac Royall, who removed, in 1737, from Antigua to Medford, and built [3] a fine mansion, which is still standing there. To this Cambridge home Penelope Vassall came as a bride, and lived here thirty-four years. Major Vassall bought of his brother John, who had made the purchase in 1747, the half-acre corner on Windmill Lane, and probably at that time built the brick wall, which has so long been a landmark to the traveller on Brattle and Ash streets. Here he died in 1769 and was buried in his tomb under Christ Church, of which he was one of the original founders.

His granddaughter, Miss Catherine G. Russell, whom the writer well re-

---

[1] Mary married Judge Richard Lechmere; Rebecca, Judge Joseph Lee; and Sarah, Andrew Boardman.

[2] It has often been said and printed, that he gave it.

[3] See Drake's *Historic Fields and Mansions*, p. 119.

members, said that Major Henry Vassall lived in the house twenty-seven years, dying here in 1769, and that his widow continued to reside here until the Revolution. Cambridge, becoming a military camp, was neither a pleasant nor safe residence for those who still adhered to King George, so that Madame Vassall departed in haste for Antigua with her only daughter, the wife of Dr. Charles Russell of Lincoln. They left so hurriedly as to carry off a young girl by the name of Moody, a relative of Sir William Pepperell, who was visiting here, and whom, on account of the state of the country, they were unable to return to her friends. She married in the West Indies, and only returned to New England on a visit many years afterwards. A strong belief prevails in Cambridge that a subterranean passage connects this house with Mr. H. W. Longfellow's, and that it was constructed to enable the two Vassall families to visit each other without exposure to the outside world. Many years ago the writer with her brothers and a brother of the Poet made a progress through the cellars in a vain search after this mysterious and mythical passage-way, one of the party only retaining a conviction that if a walled-up arch of solid masonry could be opened the entrance might be found. The story that this house is haunted has been current for several generations.

> "All houses wherein men have lived and died
> Are haunted houses."

Popular tradition asserts that the slaves of the Vassalls were inhumanly treated. There seems to be no foundation for this report, and there is documentary evidence proving Madame Vassall's kindness in paying twenty pounds, in 1722, to free the child of her servant Tony from slavery.

Tony Vassall, as he was called, had been brought from Jamaica when a boy by one of the family, and was a character well known in Cambridge, for after the departure of his mistress he and his wife Lucy lived many years on North Avenue, on the western side near Wright Street. The site of their house is still marked by a large horse-chestnut tree. In our grandmother's days he kept green the name of Vassall by his tales of their grandeur, and his own by relating the Apollo-like style in which he drove their chariot into Boston on week-days and to Christ Church, Cambridge, on Sundays. His mantle fell upon his son Darby, who of late years occasionally came out to Cambridge with his pass from Miss Russell to entitle him to honorable burial in the tomb of his old mistress; at last he died at the advanced age of ninety-two, and by a singular coincidence his body was brought out for interment on the centennial anniversary of the opening of the church, October 15, 1861. After his burial the tomb was to be forever closed.

> "At her head
> Lies a slave to attend the dead."

This estate, contrary to the generally received opinion, was never confiscated. At the breaking out of hostilities Mrs. Vassall had been for many years a widow, and her only child was a daughter, so that they could have taken no active part for the King. After her departure this large house with its numerous rooms became the head-quarters of the medical department of the army, under the care of the director-general, Dr. Benjamin Church. Here his corps of surgeons lived, and here, probably, many a brave man wounded at Bunker Hill breathed his last. Here in this very room may he have penned the letter the discovery of which caused his arrest. Here in this house, we are told by a contemporary letter, was he confined, and corroborating evidence is found on the door of this room where I write : " B. Church, Jr.," is still visible deeply cut in the wood, though for a century successive coats of paint have vainly tried to conceal or to obliterate the name of a traitor. From this house, one hundred years ago, was he taken in a chaise (perhaps one of Madame Vassall's), and to the music of a fife and drum, escorted by General Gates and a guard of twenty men to the place of his trial in Watertown meeting-house, where he was sentenced to imprisonment in a distant town, which was afterwards commuted to transportation for life. The ship in which he sailed for the West Indies was supposed to have gone down with all on board.

After the Revolution, the rights of Mrs. Vassall, and the mortgages with which the property was burdened, were purchased by Nathaniel Tracy of Newburyport, who also owned and occupied the estate of John Vassall on the opposite side of the road, where he resided in great state for a few years. This house was then occupied by Fred. Geyer, whose daughter, Marianne, married Andrew, the grandson of Governor Belcher, and his only representative in the male line.

In 1792, Andrew Cragie bought the whole property, and soon after Bossenger Foster, his brother-in-law, removed from Boston and occupied this house. The children of Mr. Foster were Andrew Cragie's heirs, and after his death, in 1821, on the division of his estate that was not subject to dower, lot No. 1, the seven acres of Major Henry Vassall, and the house, fell to Elizabeth Foster, then the wife of Judge Samuel B. Haven, of whom the present owner purchased it in 1841.

I cannot more appropriately close this article than with the following sonnet, recently written in the album of one of the young people of the family : —

> " Old house, left standing in the garden bed,
>   Whispering memories of heroic days ;
>   Idly I stand, and from thy window gaze
> On trains that creep to city of the dead.
> Idly stood Church and leaned his heavy head
>   On window panes, that shut him from the sight
>   Of rolls of honor, where men's names were bright, —
>   — He scratched his name on prison-door instead.
> The dead are dead, of body or of name

The grave holds dust, and on the record lies
  The deadly story of the name that dies.
The living live, — on earth, aspiring flame,
  In heaven, as stars that light us from the skies.
  Old house ! through thee their image fills our eyes."

ENGLISH LETTER. APRIL, 1775.

From the Sparks Cabinet, at Gore Hall, belonging to William Eliot Sparks.

A Circumstantial Account of an Attack that happened on the 19th of April 1775, on his Majesty's Troops, by a Number of the People, of the Province of Massachusetts Bay.

ON Tuesday, the 18 of April, about half past 10th at night Lieutenant Colonel Smith of the 10th Regiment, embarked from the Common at Boston, with the Grenadiers and Light-Infantry, of the Troops there, and landed on the Opposite side, from whence he began his march towards Concord. where he was ordered to destroy the Magazine of Military Stores deposited there for the use of an Army to be Assembled in Order to act against his Majesty and his Gouernment, the Colonel called his Officers together and gave orders that the troops should not fire. unless fired upon, and after Marching a few Miles. — Detached six Companies of light Infantry under the Command of Major Pitcairn to take possession of two Bridges on the other side of Concord, Soon after they heard many signal Guns, and the ringing of Alarm Bells repeatedly, which convinced them that the Country was rising to oppose them, and that it was a preconcerted Scheme to oppose the King's Troops, wheneuer there should be a favorable opportunity for it. About three O'Clock the next Morning, the Troops being advanced within two Miles of Lexington. intelligence was received that about 500 Men in Arms were Assembled and determined to oppose the King's Troops, and, on Major Pitcairn Galloping up to the Head, of the advanced Companies, two Officers informed him, that a Man (advanced from those that were Assembled) had presented his Musquet and attempted to shoot them, but the Piece flashed in the pan. — On this the Major gave directions to the Troops to move forward, but on no Account to fire, nor even to attempt it without orders. When they Arrived at the end of the Village they observed about 200 armed Men drawn up on a Green, and when the Troops came within 100 yards of them, they began to file off towards some stone walls on their right Flank : The light Infantry observing this, ran after them, the Major instantly called to the Soldiers not to fire, but to Surround and disarm them, some of whom had jumped over a Wall. then fired 4 or 5 shot at the Troops. Wounded a Man of the 10th Regiment, and the Major Howe in two places, and at the same time Several Shots were fired from a Meeting-House on the left, Upon this, without any order or regularity the Light Infantry began a Scattered Fire, and Killed seueral of the Country People, but were Silenced, as soon as the Authority of the Officers could make them.

After this Colonel Smith Marched up with the remainder of the detachment, and the whole Body proceeded to Concord, where they Arrived about Nine O'Clock, without any thing further happening; but vast Numbers of Armed People were seen Assembling on all the heights, While Colonel Smith with the Grenadiers and part of the Light Infantry, remained at Concord to search for Cannon &c there, he detached Captain Parsons, with six light Companies to secure a Bridge at some Distance from Concord, and to proceed from thence to certain houses where it was supposed there was Cannon & Ammunition, Capt. Parsons, in pursuance of these Orders, posted three Companies at the Bridge, and on some heights near it, under the Command of Captain Laurie of the 43d Regiment, and with the remainder went and destroyed some Cannon Wheels, Powder and Ball.

The People still continued encreasing on the Heights, and in about an Hour after, a Large Body of them began to Move towards the Bridge, the light Companies of the 4th & 10th then descended and joined Captain Laurie, the People continued to Advance in great Numbers, and fired upon the King's Troops, Killed three men, Wounded four Officers, one Sergeant, and four Privates, upon which (after returning the fire) Captain Laurie and his Officers, thought it prudent to retreat towards the main Body at Concord, and were soon joined by two Companies of Grenadiers; when Captain Parsons returned with the three Companies over the Bridge, they observed three Soldiers on the Ground, one of them Scalped, his head much Mangled, and his ears cut off, tho' not quite Dead: a sight which struck the Soldiers with horror: Captain Parsons Marched on and Joined the Main Body, who were only waiting for his coming up to March back to Boston. Colonel Smith had executed his Orders, without opposition, by destroying all the Military Stores he could find; both the Colonel, and Major Pitcairn having taken all possible pains to convince the Inhabitants that no Injury was intended them, and that if they Opened their doors when required to search for said Stores, not the Slightest mischief should be done, neither had any of the People the least occasion to Complain; but they were Sulky, and one of them euen struck Major Pitcairn. — Except upon Captain Laurie at ye Bridge no Hostilities happened, from the Affair at Lexington, until the Troops began their March back. — As soon as the Troops had got out of the Town of Concord they received a heavy fire on them from all sides, from Walls. Fences. Houses. Trees. Barns. &c. which continued without intermission, till they Met the first Brigade, with two field Pieces, near Lexington, Ordered out, under the Command of Lord Percy, to support them; advice having been receiued about seuen O'Clock next Morn-

English Letter.

ing, that Signals had been made, and expresses gone out to alarm the Country, and that the People were rising to attack the Troops under Colonel Smith : Upon the Firing of the Field Pieces, the People's Fire was for a while silenced, but as they still continued to increase greatly in Numbers they fired again as before from all Places where they could find cover, upon the whole Body, and continued so doing for the space of 15 miles. Notwithstanding their numbers, they did not attack openly during the whole Day, but kept under couer on all occasions. The Troops were uery much fatigued, the greater part of them having been under Arms all Night and made a March of upwards of 40 Miles before they arrived at Charlestown, from whence they were ferryed over to Boston. —

The Troops had above Fifty Killed. and many more wounded. Reports are various about the loss sustained by the Country People Some make it uery considerable, others not so much.

Thus this unfortunate Affair has happened thro' the rashness and impudence of a few People who began firing on the Troops at Lexington. — *Contributed by* MRS. M. C. SPARKS.

LETTERS OF EDMUND QUINCY.

Furnished by Miss Donnison.

To Y^e Rev^d Mr. Jacob Bigelow.

LANR *June* 18, 1776 —

Dr. Sir. I recd y^r favor of y^e 5th a few days since & am pleased with hearing Mrs. B. is satisfied with Eunice [1] her conduct : & hope may continue, & that Mrs. B. will testify her regards in suitable instruction of a spiritual as well as temporal nature, & thereby increase her expected serviceableness — I'm disappointed in ye girl's failing in ye faculty of milking w^h she was used to at Mr. B's : possibly instruction and practise may conquer the difficulty. *Labor improbus omnia vincit* — you'll suppose, as I do, ye Girl will want some supply of money, I ask ye favor of Mrs. B to see that the most prudent application be made. We are now publicly alarmed with the B. naval & land force expected ag^t ye city & county of N. Y: perhaps it may be begun ; it will, I hope, under ye irresistible decrees of D : P : prove ye means of opening ye eyes of ye B. Court & nation, & even of flashing conviction before them, that there is an impregnable Barrier now raised & fix^t between their cruel as well as hostile designs, and the late feeble & unprepared Col^o of America — wh. I think by the will of Heaven are fast rising into States, wh. under ye protection of ye God of Armies, may become objects of ye closest European attention & commercial attraction : and these things seem not to be very distant.

The probability of a full native supply of every needed warlike article of defence by sea & land is a distinguishing circumstance, wh. ye nations will early mark out. As a fundamental cause of ye future growth of ye No. A. States : & ye strife will be, wh. European powers will avail themselves most of their future commerce, should ye Fla. of war be confined to Europe, *each* will be fond of furnishing their manuf^{es} to these, as they suppose, unprovided & incapable Americans : but on ye other hand, ye latter, if not blinded, will choose & labor to provide themselves with materials & manufactures as fast as they need them : for every needed community, & as to ye superfluous, it is to be supposed, that each state, will by law, discourage ye importation by heavy duties — Altho. we have a country, (I mean the

---

[1] A colored woman owned by E. Q.

United Provinces) capable of almost every European production & abounding in more extensive native productions than any K. dom & perhaps all in Europe, we must, nevertheless, endeavor to imitate the wise example of ye 7 United prov^s of Holl^d after ye revolt from Spain & during their 30 years war with that *then* powerful Kingdom.

We must promote agriculture, manufactures, industry & economy & above all cultivate Religion & Virtue May the Giver of peace grant these U. States a series of peaceful years & that by means thereof ye American heathen may be bro't ye saving Knowledge of ye True God.

These will even be ye subject of ye earnest supplications of ye faithful thro' ye gospelized regions of No. America.

I am with my best wishes to you and y^r household Sir, &c. —

P. S. By last advice we have now in our hands abt, 700 of those Highlanders w^h ye Brit Adm^on at an immense expense deceived last year with a promise of their being sent to A. to take possession of ye evacuated estates of those who they were told had fled back 100 miles & more into ye wilderness, through ye terror of ye Brit. arms &c. w^h ye Captives now acquaint us with, standing astonished at ye falsity of ye facts w^h they were made to believe some appearing very *morose* under ye disap^t & others well en^o satisfied — you'll have read of ye absolute refusal of ye Ld Howe to take command of ye ministerial naval force to ye sing^r mortification of the ministry & doubtless of their *Head.* It is improbable his lordship was of opinion, that one Bro^r was enough to share y^e *Infamy* wh. he had become sensible would prove ye result of ye ministerial proceedings Pray God ye final issue may graduate with his L^dships just apprehension! However it's probable he may soon have work nearer home as they are doubtless on the verge of a European Breach — A farmer would be very remarkable who would set his dogs to worry his sheep, while his neighbors cattle were breaking into his fields, ye fences having become indefensible.

LAN^R *June* 24, 1776

TO THE H^BLE J. HANCOCK ESQ.

Dr Sir. I hope ere this Mr Bant with my Dr K. has had ye pleasure of seeing you & Dr H. well at P. By ye Cont^ls L^r of advice to ye convent^o at N. Y. we are daily expecting adv. of a Min^l Fleet & army being before that city & a siege begun. Letters from H^x of 5th curr^t inform us that no Fleet had arrived there to that day, but that it was very sickly in ye F army & navy, that many refugees of Yr^o B^o had died, among wh^m were named F Lillie & wife & Mr. J. Fitch his eldest d^r & that F : lay at ye point of death. It is doubtless a very mel^ly time in that Asylum of of ye B. troops & th^r Fr^ds Y^r may have rec^d odr^s fro Europe w^h may give you insight into the causes by w^h ye min^l proceedings have been embar^rd & their grand Armament delayed — here we are left to our own conjectures.

you'll be ad^{vd} probably ere this reaches you, that by batteries *at length* erected, near ye en^{tr} of B^o Harbor — Com^o Bank's ship & his convoy had been obliged to make a precipitate flight ab^t 10 days ago, & that several ships with Highlanders have been drove and carried in by our privateers, not fewer in no. than 4 or 500 — great part of whom have been bro't into ye several towns & more expected, in order to ease ye Cha. of their support & to prevent mischief. It is expected we may hear of more arrivals of troops at B^o as to an attack upon it, I'm not much concerned, if, as I'm told their fortifications are compleated in a defensible manner.

When Comm^o Banks lay in the harbour, a Cont^l Privateer having been taken & bro't under his care, it gave occasion for a Flag of truce to go on bord for exchange of prisoners — ye business being ended, ye afflicted Comm^o ment^d to ye Co. ye disastrous att^a of his boats on Capt. Muckford of Mbh. & another p. of only 7 men on board — He told them he had lost 63 of his best off^{ers} & men : supposing that a part of them were in our hands, & said he hoped they treated Lt Banks well. They replying that they had heard of no such person being bro't among them, B. appeared vastly concerned saying that he had then lost his brother & 1st Lt. & one of his best off^{rs} in ye navy — however we hear a corps was found upon the beach some days since & supposed to be that of ye person mentioned by B. — it being clad well with a pr. of pistols, a hanger, some money in ye pockets & a gold watch. It is said that not more than 30 men were on board the 2 privateers wh. if fact, & also that they were unexpectedly attackt it would argue much courage in the defenders, one of w^h Capt. B. told them he wanted to know the name of as having proved himself a bold & stout man, in beheading one of his boat's crew looking over the gunwale of the privateer with one stroke of his broad sword saying to ye even in ye fisherman's dialect, " I've taken off his head, you may gut him." By such men ye character of American prowess is fast advancing. I hear by a friend from B^o that ye Highlanders, especially ye officers may have appeared morose & ill tempered imagining they had got among unpolished people till ye fun^l rites were prepared of their Major killed by one of the privateers, who was decently interred by mil^{ty} honor, attended by a no. of our off^{ers} & ye inhabitants — after which these strangers seemed to think they had go into a good country * * * * 10 guineas a head were paid them at listing, after 6 mos. imprisonment they were embarqued — several hundred deserted after enlistment on hearing that no evacuation of Estates had been heard of in it, so that their expectations would be frustrated. We are still without any certain advice how things stand in Canada, but we are too well assured of some of y^e *Min^l Cash* having lately operated on Sev^l of ye Cont^l officers — I presume ere this come to hand ye Cong^s may have rec^d from ye sev^{ral} Col^o their assent to a speedy Declaration of Independence upon & a total disconnection, with the Gov. of G. B.

I hope this may meet you in ye enjoyment of such a degree of health as may enable you to sustain ye wg^t of ye present public incumbrance —
With my kind regards to my Daughters
I re^m very sincerely D. Sir, your
Aff. & obliged Fnd & Fath^r

P. S. 29 This going open for want of conv'y'nce we have adv from N. Y. of more than 100 conspirators there in Gaol for a design on y^e Gen^{ls} life & also for blowing up 30 tuns of powder — a plot similar to that of 1588 & I think a similar fate ought to be the portion of y^e present conspirators.

THE RIVER CHARLES IN JUNE.
BY JAMES RUSSELL LOWELL.

      The sliding Charles,
Blue toward the West, and bluer and more blue,
Living and lustrous as a woman's eyes.
Look once and look no more, with southward curve
Ran crinkling sunniness, like Helen's hair
Glimpsed in Elysium, insubstantial gold;
From blossom-clouded orchards, far away
The bobolink tinkled; the deep meadows flowed
With multitudinous pulse of light and shade
Against the bases of the southern hills,
While here and there a drowsy island rick
Slept and its shadow slept; the wooden bridge
Thundered, and then was silent; on the roofs
The sun-warped shingles rippled with the heat;
Summer on field and hill, in heart and brain,
All life washed clean in this high tide of June.
        From "Under the Willows."

OLD CAMBRIDGE.

Know old Cambridge? Hope you do. —
Born there? Don't say so! I was, too . . . .
— Nicest place that ever was seen, —
Colleges red, and Common green,
Sidewalks brownish with trees between.
Sweetest spot beneath the skies
When the canker-worms don't rise, —
When the dust, that sometimes flies
Into your mouth and ears and eyes,
In a quiet slumber lies,
Not in the shape of unbaked pies
Such as barefoot children prize.
      DR. O. W. HOLMES.

  Dear native town! whose choking elms each year
  With eddying dust before their time turn gray,
    Pining for rain, — to me thy dust is dear;
  It glorifies the eve of summer day,
    And when the westering sun half-sunken burns,
    The mote-thick air to deepest orange turns,
  The westward horseman rides through clouds of gold away.
      JAMES RUSSELL LOWELL.

THE OLD COURT HOUSE.

BY JOHN HOLMES.

THE old Court House, which stood on the site of the present Lyceum, was built from the timbers of the meeting-house which was replaced in 1756 by that which was demolished in 1833.[1]

The beams, joists, and rafters which had so often heard the Law and its works depreciated from a theological point of view, were now to recognize the Law in another sense, as the stern presiding spirit of the place. They were now to see whether the people would in this transformed building, attend as strictly to their temporal interests as they had before done to their spiritual.

While the colonial dependence lasted, it would seem that the judges of the Superior Court, coming to hold their sessions here, were received at the county or town line by the sheriff and attendant gentlemen, and escorted in state to their lodgings,[2] which, in this case, being interpreted, probably means Bradish's Tavern, on the present Brighton Street. If we listen, we hear break on the quiet of the past, the rumble of wheels and the thump of hoofs making mild thunder on Brighton Bridge. While Cambridge was yet a village, this was the sound that late in the night warned the wakeful of a new arrival, and by its cadence, allowed him to guess whether it were the village doctor returning from a call extraordinary, or a courier panting to tell of success or disaster at Lake George.

We behold the commotion as of to-day. The villagers quit their gray, unpainted houses, as if they were in flames. Children get the start. Women peer from the windows, or group on door-steps, and snatch a breath of respite from their unending cares. Austere men who combat the world and its pleasures, move slowly forth, go circuitously and drop (as it were), casually and unconsciously into the throng. Suitors and sued, witnesses summoned for the term, amateurs of litigation who have had their losses, — the many who love the mysteries of the civil, and doat on the dread forms of the criminal process, — poor debtors, who "swear out" from time to time,

---

[1] Our authority is the Rev. Lucius R. Paige, who, beside other motives, has now that of self-defence, to finish his *History of Cambridge*, so numerous are the local questions put to him which he kindly answers.

[2] Washburn's *Judicial History of Massachusetts*.

and who know every spider in the Old Jail (near Winthrop Square), and every mullein and thistle in its yard, and who, from long habit, scrutinize the world in small portions as through grated windows, — all these contribute to the variety of the crowd.

The "Scholars" (to use the popular term some fifty years since) are hurrying to the scene of action, the banyan (such as Prescott wore at Bunker Hill) floating wide behind them as they run. This garment, a long calico dressing-gown, was still popular in summer so late as 1820.

Bradish stands at his door, grave and portly. His cue, newly bound with black ribbon, hangs perpendicular, like a pendulum stopped by earthquake.

What ceremonies attended the opening of the court we cannot say, but the judges doubtless wore their "robes of scarlet English cloth, their broad bands, and their immense judicial wigs,"[1] and probably the barristers appeared "in their bands, gowns, and tyewigs."[2]

We think we may have beheld the "last attenuation" of judicial pomp, in seeing the late Chief Justice Shaw going from the court to his dinner, accompanied (not preceded) by the sheriff alone. The latter carried in an easy way a long, light wand (using it, we think, somewhat like a cane), in which lay, we suppose, like latent caloric, the protective, vindictive, and remedial power of the Commonwealth.

Here Sewall, Hutchinson, and Lynde presided, and here attended the great colonial lawyers, Pratt, Gridley, Trowbridge, and the rest. Special pleading was in its full vigor. It was a stern, compulsory system of statement and argument, designed to lead by the shortest way, to an issue of law or fact, to be decided by the Court or the jury. No such theory, submitted to the working of strong hands, fails to be more or less warped out of shape, and this had undoubtedly its share of subtlety and finesse. If one of those old law practitioners were compelled to revisit earth for a term, he would find no better reading than the "quiddits and quillets," filed in our Court House at that day.

The lawyers were then, as they are now, the gladiators of a better civilization.

After the Revolution, Chief Justices Dana and Parsons presided here at the sessions of the Supreme Court. The latter lodged during the session at a house, which, if it were standing, would be the third building on the left-hand side of Brighton Street, north from Mount Auburn Street. Here the great lawyer diverted himself in the evening, with what other men might deem labor. An old member of the bar who lodged here has often told us with complacency of his evening colloquies with the Chief Justice. Dexter, H. G. Otis, and other well known lawyers represented the new republican bar.

In or about 1815, the courts were removed to East Cambridge, and the Court House ceased from its former functions.

[1] John Adams, from Washburn's *Judicial History of Massachusetts*.   [2] Same.

The Court of Probate was still occasionally held here by the late Judge Fay.

Town meetings, which had been held here for an indefinite time, were, in 1831, transferred to the then new City Hall, on Main Street, in Cambridgeport.

When the division took place in the First Parish, the Court House was occupied for Sunday worship until the Orthodox Church on Mount Auburn Street was completed.

Lyceum lectures and debates were begun here about 1830, and held their ground with very considerable tenacity. The public finally became satiated and dropped off in something like a comatose state. The great variety of subjects, and the distractions of a social surrounding, left, it is to be feared, a rather nebulous result on the general mind.

Cambridge had been for many years remarkably exempt from fires. From near 1812, we recall from hearsay or observation, no serious fire. The town therefore was obliged to borrow its excitement on this score from neighboring calamities. And to judge by the demonstrations, the sufferers themselves could hardly have felt the situation more intensely than our citizens. The parish bell was immediately set going, nor ceased while any faint gleam of light appeared on the horizon. Nearly all the male inhabitants cried fire incessantly for some half hour. The "scholars" lent their lungs to assist the town. The engine rushed madly though heavily out into space, and returned. One got to feel as if this were a beneficial operation. The alarm bell actually suggested security. When it rung out with the greatest vigor, and for the longest time, the householder knew that the fire was very distant, and that our conscientious citizens could not relax their efforts while the flames appeared, or were reflected on the sky.

But in October, 1839, a fire actually occurred within our own precincts, which consumed three houses and a barn, and, as usual, threatened much more destruction. At the beginning of the following winter, a suspicion arose that incendiaries were preparing to repeat, on a comprehensive scale, the calamity of October.

We can recollect no cause assigned for the new alarm, and possibly the imagination worked with more effect, uncontrolled by specific evidence. It was soon found that a citizens' patrol was necessary to protect the town. It was arranged, and fixed its head-quarters in the old Court House. We recollect only a tendency to hilarity that pervaded the organization, at variance with the imminent hazard which they labored to avert. Walking, watching, and friendly converse occupied the midnight hours. Consciousness of merit, was the pure and honorable reward of our exertions. No refreshments were furnished to dilute or vitiate this noble sensation.

We infer the greatness of the impending danger, from the great and general effort made to avert it. And it is a memorable fact, that so extensive and desperate a confederation of incendiaries should have been entirely crushed by our demonstration. Perfect incombustibility seemed to prevail during this period, and in a community, too, where one man in twenty was a probable Guy Faux.

There is always one drawback on precaution, — that it cuts off the very evidence that should justify it. The patrol of 1840 were subject to this inconvenience.

Only one arrest was made. It was of a man who at a very early hour of the morning was detected carrying incendiary material toward the college. He was seized with his lantern and his various pyrotechnics, carried to the Court House, and subjected to severe examination. He proved to be a professional incendiary, *i. e.*, a fire maker in the college. His trial, though in a measure *pro forma*, gave an aspect of efficiency to the patrol, and added to its moral strength. The dullest intellect perceived what might have occurred, had the prisoner been one of the real confederates, and had no patrol existed to arrest his deadly career.

No monument or inscription commemorates the services of that time, not even a bronze extinguisher of minute size.

Among the members of the patrol, rheumatism, cough, and catarrh may have done their work, but no voice has proclaimed the fact. Wide awake beneficence disdains to stir sleeping gratitude, but any member of the patrol may proudly say, pointing to the unconsumed town, *Circumspice*.

In 1841, the old Court House was sold, and was removed back to the west side of the present Palmer Street. Here it was at first used for a billiard room and bowling alley; next for a gymnasium and fencing school, then (on the lower floor, — having been changed to a two-story building) for furniture — then on the same floor for hardware. It was removed within a year or two to the west side of Palmer Street, and made to adjoin Whitney's Block, with which it communicates. The lower floor is at present occupied by a "Holly Tree Coffee Shop," the upper by the Social Union, kindly and wisely conducted by those to whose modest merit we pay the unusual compliment of omitting their names.

THE LAMENT OF THE WEATHERCOCK OF 1776.

"Carmina jam moriens canit exequialia [*gallus*]." — OVID, *Met.* XIV. 430.

"He makes a swan-like end,
Fading in music." — SHAKESPEARE.

At midnight's solemn hour I woke; —
The moon all brightly shone;
I rose, and donned my old plaid cloak,
And wandered forth alone.

The air was still, — no sound nor noise, —
The air all silent, too;
When an unearthly, piercing voice
Cried, "Cock-a-doodle-doo!"

I started, and my knees did knock
Together, in my fear,
For 't was the ancient weathercock
That startled thus my ear.

Thrice did he flap his wings, and crow,
Ere he the words could bring;
Then, as I trembling stood below,
'T was thus I heard him sing : —

"Farewell to thee, old Cambridge! Farewell to each and all!
I 'm doomed to an ignoble fate, and an untimely fall.
Farewell, my pleasant, airy home! my heart is big with sorrow,
To think, thou dear old steeple! that we must part to-morrow.
And the people that once loved us must also from us part; —
They 've built a grand new church and spire, surmounted by a dart;
That gaudy, glittering arrow, that I can plainly see,
Is ever striving with the wind, to aim itself at me.

"Farewell to *thee*, old Harvard! Peace be within thy walls!
Sound learning and true wisdom aye flourish in thy halls!
No more may I behold thy courts and corners all alive
With little black-coats, buzzing round, like bees about a hive;

The Lament of the Weathercock of 1776.

No more may I behold their troops in mock militia muster,
Nor see them on the parting day around the old elm cluster.
The last Commencement Day, it was a bitter day to me,
For I felt that it must be the last I evermore should see;
And my old friend, the Phi Beta! I can scarce restrain my tears,
For the music of thy last sweet song is ringing in my ears.

"Alas! the meeting-house and I have doubtless had our day;
And the spoiler comes to-morrow to take us both away.
But we 'll not depart in anger, nor will I much repine
That this exalted station can be no longer mine.
My conscience bears me witness, that ever, from my youth,
I 've lived an upright weathercock, and always told the truth.
My life has been a long, and I hope a useful one;
And now I droop my crest, and am ready to be gone."

Thrice did he flap his wings, and crow,
When he his song had done;
Then, wondering, homewards did I go,
Just as the clock struck one.

December 22, 1833.

These lines were written by Mrs. Charles Folsom, when the old meeting-house was taken down. The "last sweet song," mentioned in the sixth stanza, was Mr. Longfellow's Phi Beta Kappa poem. — ED.

PRAISE OF THE PAST.

BY GEORGE PARSONS LATHROP.

OF ancient days how manifold
    The harvests here around us grown!
What fruits we hold, by valiant-souled
    And simple farmer-heroes sown!

They, while they learned the bullet's creed
    No less in solemn worship kneeled;
By faith and deed they spread the seed
    Of peace and strength in every field; —

And ours the rich maturity,
    While over us, afar and near,
That broad-arched tree, the century,
    Spreads wide its branches, each a year!

Ah well, how swiftly things disperse :
    In how much changed are place and time!
For poets rehearse their dulcet verse
    Where patriot-spurs once clinked in rhyme;

The city spreads its ravages ;
    The grace of older growth is fled :
Hills bow their knees, prone lie the trees,
    Faith, too, they say, is long since dead.

Yet with our fathers we are one
    At heart, whatever change betide,
Still shines for us their tireless sun :
    Their truth still waits us for our guide.

And we, though larger grows the scope
    Of vision, now, toward God and man,
From broader hope gaze back Time's slope
    To praise their virtue's narrower plan.

Oh, when our crumbling lives have gone,
  Shall others unto us look back
O'er deeps that yawn, and see our dawn
  Glow pure behind their devious track?

Who knows? We live in veering days.
  Yet o'er all fame our deeds may hold,
Fair shines this praise, this record stays:—
  WE DID NOT LET THE PAST GROW OLD!

A PARTIAL LIST OF AUTHORITIES CONSULTED IN PREPARING THIS BOOK.

Colburn. Bibliography of the Local History of Massachusetts.
Palfrey. History of New England.
Hubbard. History of New England.
Holmes. History of Cambridge.
Wood. New England's Prospect.
Dudley. Letter to the Countess of Lincoln.
Mather. Magnalia.
Johnson. Wonder-Working Providence in New England.
Prince. New England Chronology.
Winthrop. History of New England.
Newell. Discourse on the Cambridge Church Gathering in 1636.
Lives of the Chief Fathers of New England, vol. vi. The Life of Thos. Hooker, by Edw. W. Hooker, vol. iv.
The Life of Thos. Shepard, by John A. Albro.
Hudson. — History of Lexington.
Jackson. History of Newton.
Bond. Genealogies and History of Watertown.
Nason. Gazetteer of Massachusetts.
John Dunton. Letters from New England.
Hutchinson. History of Massachusetts.
Barry. History of Massachusetts.
Drake. Historic Fields and Mansions of Middlesex.
Drake. Old Landmarks and Historical Personages of Boston.
Hoppin. Historical Notice of Christ Church.
Clarke and Force. American Archives.
Journals of each Provincial Congress of Massachusetts in 1774 and 1775, and of the Committee of Safety.
Frothingham. Siege of Boston.
Records of the Massachusetts Bay Colony.
Town Records of Cambridge.
Bancroft. History of United States.
Frost. Pictorial History of United States.
Willard. Republic of America.
Marshall. Life of Washington.
Sparks. Writings of Washington.

Quincy. History of Harvard College.
S. A. Eliot. History of Harvard College.
Griswold. The Republican Court.
Sabine. Loyalists of the American Revolution.
Amory. Old Cambridge and New.
Simpson. Two Hundred Years Ago.
Letters of John Adams.
Letters of Mrs. Adams.
Homes of American Authors.
Madame Riedesel's Memoir and Letters.
McKenzie. History of the First Church of Cambridge.
McKenzie. Washington in Cambridge, "Atlantic Monthly," July, 1875.
McKenzie. Memorial Address on Cambridge Men who fell at Lexington.
Tracy. Great Awakening.
Wells. Life and Public Services of Samuel Adams.
Duyckinck. National Portrait Gallery of Eminent Americans.
Dawson. Correspondence on the Character of General Israel Putnam.
Dawson. Diary of David Howe.
Phelps. History of Newgate of Connecticut.
Curwen. Journal and Letters.
Parton. Life of Aaron Burr.
Trumbull. Reminiscences of His Own Times.
Bridgman. Epitaphs from Copp's Hill Burying Ground, Boston.
Harris. Epitaphs from the Old Burying Ground, Cambridge.
Peabody. Centennial Address at Cambridge, July 3, 1875.
Hawthorne. Twice-told Tales.
Hale. One Hundred Years Ago.
Clarke and Vaille. The Harvard Book.
Washburn. Judicial History of Massachusetts.
Greene. Life of Nathanael Greene.
Sibley. Biographical Sketches of Graduates of Harvard University.
Sibley. Manuscript Collections.

INDEX.

ADAMS, John, 32, 61, 88.
Adams, John, his hopes, 15.
Adams, John, in Cambridge, 53.
Adams, Mrs. John, in Cambridge, 42.
Adams, Samuel, 23, 33, 54.
Amen, Dr. Appleton's, 31.
Ammunition, The lack of, 12, 26, 27.
Appleton, Rev. Dr., 31, 49, 59, 62, 72, 80.
Apthorp, The Rev. East, 10, 50, 51.
Apthorp house, 21, 50.
Apthorp, Mad. Grizzel, 51.
Army, The New Continental, 51.
Arnold, Benedict, 37, 55.
Authorities, List of, 119.

Batchelder house, see (*Henry*) *Vassall house*.
Belcher, Jonathan, 95, 97; Arms, 95.
Belknap, Dr. Jeremy, 39, 91.
Bigelow, Rev. Jacob, 106.
Borland house, see *Apthorp house*.
Boston, becomes the Capital, 24; besieged, 26. distress in, 21; evacuated, 59.
Bradish Tavern, 18, 75, 111.
Brattle Arms, The, 90.
Brattle grounds, 75.
Brattle house, 35.
Brattle's Mall, 43.
Brewster house, see *Sewall House*.
British fleet leaves Boston, 81.
Bunker Hill, 13, 24, 29.
Burgoyne, Gen., 23.
Burr, Aaron, 28, 33, 37.
Butler's (Dana) Hill, 31, 74.
Byles, Mather, 70.

Caghnawaga Indians in Cambridge, 53.
Calef, Robert, his book burned, 48.
Cambridge commerce, 28.
Cambridge, its influence in 1776, 12; its territory, 5; sketch of, 3.
Camp diet in Cambridge, 58.

Canada, expedition to, 36, 55.
Caner, Dr., 51, 65.
Charles river in June, 110.
Chauncy, President Charles, 35, 46.
Christ Church, 11, 29, 49.
Church, Benj., 37, 80, 101; condemned, 40; his traitorous correspondence, 37.
Church Row, 77.
Clergy, The, 14.
Clinton, Gen., 23.
Cobble Hill, now Somerville, 41.
Cold, in the church, 57.
Colonies, The thirteen, 51.
"Common Sense," 54.
Congratulations addressed to Washington, 61, 62.
Congress, The first provincial, 10.
Copp's Hill, 66, 70.
Correspondence, Epistolary, decaying, 36.
Court House, The, 72, 111.
Cragie, Andrew, 101.
Cragie house, see (*John*) *Vassall house*.
Crime in camp, 43.

Dana Hill (Butler's Hill), 31.
Dana house, 74.
Dankers and Sleyter visit Harvard, 47.
Declaration of Independence anticipated in Cambridge, 80.
Donnison, Miss, 106.
Dorchester Heights occupied, 59.
"Dorothy Q," 32, 84.
Downing, George, 44.
Dudley, Dorothy, her diary, 18.
Dudley, Thomas, 13.
Dunster house, 75.
Dunster, Rev. Henry, 45.

Eaton, Nathaniel, 45.
Edwards, Timothy, 32.
Eliot, John, 8.
Elm, The Washington, 16, 26.

Episcopacy in Cambridge, 9.
Evacuation of Boston, 69, 83.

Faculty of Harvard organized, 48.
Fast Day, 27, 59.
Fayerweather house, see *Ruggles house*.
Faneuil Hall, 65; used as a theatre, 53.
Fires in Cambridge, 113.
Flag, The Union, 51.
Fleet, The British, sails from Boston, 61.
Fort Number One, 75.
Franklin, Benjamin, 23, 37, 40, 54, 91.
Frizzle, John, 97.
Frost, Mr., 77.

Gage, Gen., 10, 21, 22, 37.
Gale, Theophilus, 46.
Gates, Gen. Horatio, 26.
Gates, Mr., 49.
General Court in Cambridge, 9.
Green Dragon Tavern, 65.
Greene, Gardner, 64.
Greene, Gen., 40, 52, 67, 90.
Guests at Head-Quarters, The, 89.

Hancock house, Boston, 64.
Hancock, John, 23, 32, 50, 52, 84, 107.
Hancock, Mrs. Dorothy, 32.
Hancock, Mrs. Lydia, 32.
Harvard College, 7, 14, 15, 29; removed to Concord, 20; sketch of, 44, 48.
Harvard College, its buildings, 72, 76.
Harvard Hall, burned, 48.
Haskins, D. G., Jr., 3.
Hastings house, 20.
Haynes, John, 4.
Head-quarters, see (*John*) *Vassall house*, 7.
Heath, Gen., 60.
Hessians, to be hired, 52.
Hicks, John, 19.
Hoar, Leonard, President, 46.
Hobgoblin Hall, Medford, 42.
Holly Tree Coffee Shop, 114.
Holmes house, see *Hastings house*.
Holmes, John, 111.
Holmes, O. W., 110.
Holyoke, Edward, 48.
Hooker, Rev. Thomas, 4.
Howe, Gen., 23, 37, 41, 52, 59, 60, 83.
Hutchinson, Mrs. Anne, 5.
Hutchinson, Thomas, 66.

Independence declared, 87.
Inman house, 31, 74, 75.
Inman, Ralph, 74.

Jackson, Edmund, 84.

Jail, The, 75.
Jefferson, Thomas, 87.

King's Chapel, 65.
Knox, Gen. H., 68.

Langdon, Samuel, 15, 23, 48, 57, 82.
Lechmere's Point, 40, 58.
Lechmere, Richard, 50, 78.
Lee, Charles, 26, 42, 89.
Lee house, 78.
Lee, Judge Joseph, 31, 50.
Lee, Richard Henry, 87.
Leverett, John, 48.
Lexington, 28.
Lexington, The Battle of, from a British point of view, 103.
Liberty Tree, Boston, 63.
Lincoln, Benjamin, 81.
Livingston, Robert, 37.
Locke, Samuel, 48.
Longfellow house, see (*John*) *Vassall house*.
Longfellow, H. W., 31, 66, 100.
Lowell house, see *Oliver house*.
Lowell, J. R., 110.

Manifesto of Congress, 17, 27.
Manly, Capt., captures the *Nancy*, 42.
Marcy, William, 19.
Mather, Cotton, 44, 66.
Mather, Rev. Increase, 46, 66.
Menotomy Road, 3, 77.
Mifflin, Major Thomas, 26, 35, 40, 42, 53, 90.
Montgomery, Gen. Richard, 37, 55.
Mugford, Capt., 80.
Murray, Elizabeth, 74.
Murray, James, 74.

Newe Towne, the first name of Cambridge, 3, 94.
Nichols house, see *Lee house*.
Noble, Rev. Mr., of Newburyport, preaches, 57.
North Church, Boston, 47, 65.

Old President's house, see *Wadsworth house*.
Old South Church, 63.
Oliver house, 25, 79.
Oliver, Thomas (Lt. Gov.), 40, 50.
Otis, James, 48.

Paige, Rev. Lucius R., 111.
Paine, Thomas, 54.
Patriotic resolution passed in Cambridge, 80.
Patrol of citizens, 113.
Peabody, The Rev. A. P., 12.
Pemberton Hill, Boston, 63.
Percy, Lord, 18.
Phipps house, 21, 25, 31, 75.

Index.

Phipps, Lt. Gov., 99.
Pitcairn, Maj., 36, 103.
Powder, Want of, 31.
Praise of the Past, 115.
Prescott, Col., 23, 29, 112.
Printing-press, The first, 7.
Province House, The, 63.
Putnam, Gen. Israel, 22, 26, 41, 42, 52, 69, 90.

Quebec attacked, 55.
Quincy, Dorothy, 32.
Quincy, Edmund, 50, 84; Letters of, 106, 107.
Quincy, Katy, 67, 84, 86, 107.

Richardson, Moses, 29, 77.
Riedesel house, see *Sewall house*.
Riverside Press, 75.
Recruiting in Cambridge, 41.
Regicides, The, in Cambridge, 9.
Reed, Col. Joseph, 26, 46, 90.
Remington, Judge, 97.
Revere, Paul, 63, 65, 66.
Royall, Isaac, 42, 99.
Ruggles, George, 31.
Ruggles house, 25, 31, 79.
Rules of Harvard, 46.
Rush, Benjamin, 54.
Russell, Catherine G. 99.

Sibley, Rev. John Langdon, his Sketches of Harvard Graduates, 45, 95.
Simsbury, Conn., 43.
Serjeant, The Rev. Winwood, 20, 31, 50, 77.
Sewall house, 31, 50, 78.
Sewall, Jonathan, 31, 50, 72.
Shaw, Chief Justice, 112.
Shepard Memorial Church, 46.
Shepard, Rev. Thomas, 5, 46.
Small-pox in Boston, 60.
Social Union, The, 114.
Soden Farm, 27.
"Spada," Gen. Lee's dog, 42.
Sparks, William Eliot, 103.
Sparks, Mrs. M. C., 105.
Stark, Gen., 21, 68.
St. Patrick's Day, 83.
Stone, Rev. Samuel, 4.
Students return from Concord, 82.

Sullivan, Gen., 56, 61, 68.
Synod of 1646, at Cambridge, 8.

Tea, not used, 67.
Temple, Robert, 50.
Ten Hills Farm, Somerville, 50.
Thomas, Gen., 53.
Thompson, Capt., 18.
Thompson, Col., 40.
Ticonderoga, 22.
Tobacco smoking at Harvard, 47.
Tories in Cambridge, 17, 21.
Tory families, and their rela.ionships, 50.
Tory Row, 77.
Trumbull, Major John, 26.

Vassall, Henry, 99.
Vassall house (Henry), 21, 25, 31, 34, 39, 75, 77, 93.
Vassall house (John), 31, 55, 77, 89.
Vassall, Col. John, 89, 98.
Vassall, Tony, 77, 100.
Visit, a, to Boston, 62.

Wadsworth, Benjamin, 48.
Wadsworth house, 16, 74.
Waldo, Cornelius, 78.
Waldo, Daniel, 78.
Watertown Road, 93.
Walton, Capt., 77.
Ward, Gen. Artemas, 26, 50, 62.
Warren, Gen. Joseph, 19, 22, 24.
Washington, Gen. George, 11, 15, 25, 53, 61, 62; forbids games of chance, 57; his habits, 92; his exactness in accounts, 56; original letter of, 56; in Christ Church, 49; thanked by Congress, 83.
Washington, Mrs. Martha, 55; her levee, 69.
Wells house, see *Ruggles house*.
West End, The, of Cambridge, 93.
Whitefield Elm, 76.
Whitefield, The Rev. George, in Cambridge, 79.
Wigglesworth house, 73, 74.
Windmill Hill, 94.
Winthrop, Gov., 3, 45.
Winthrop house, see *Phipps house*.
Winthrop, Mrs. Dr., 29.
Woodbridge, Rev. B., 44.

www.ingramcontent.com/pod-product-compliance
Lightning Source LLC
Chambersburg PA
CBHW070455090426
42735CB00012B/2568